The Weight of the Ice
The Northeast Ice Storm of 2008

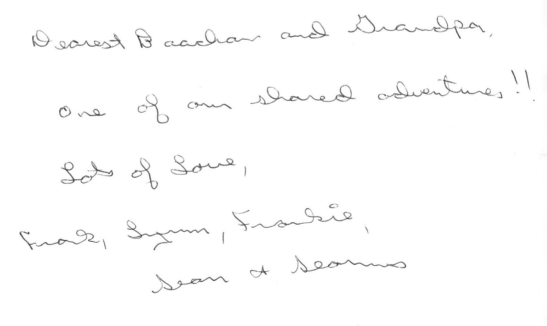

Dearest Baachan and Grandpa,

One of our shared adventures!!

Lots of Love,

Frank, Lynn, Frankie,
Sean & Seamus

31 December 2010

The Weight of the Ice
The Northeast Ice Storm of 2008

Dave Eisenstadter

Surry Cottage Books
Keene, New Hampshire

The Weight of the Ice
The Northeast Ice Storm of 2008
By Dave Eisenstadter

ISBN: 978-0-9795067-7-2

First Edition
Third Printing

Cataloging Information

Eisenstadter, Dave
The Weight of the Ice: The Northeast Ice Storm of 2008
p. cm.
Includes index
1. Natural Disasters - New England - History
QC984.N35
974.2 EISEN

Cover designed by Michel Newkirk
Cover photo by Doris Burke, PSNH
Background photo by Massey and Tomlinson Photography
Back cover photo by Jeff Newcomer

Surry Cottage Books
800 Park Avenue
Keene NH 03431
(603) 499-6500
www.surrycottagebooks.com

For mom and dad,
who lose power
whenever anyone sneezes

A snapped utility pole in Manchester, New Hampshire, on December 13.

Table of Contents

Ordinary branches are works of crystal art, like this twig in Leicester, Massachusetts.

A transformed landscape outside a window in Nelson, New Hampshire, on December 12.

Preface

By Jane Eklund
Programs Information Officer,
New Hampshire State Council on the Arts

I woke up early the morning of December 14, 2008, stiff, cold, exhausted, and cranky after a night spent on an air mattress in front of the fireplace, having risen every hour or so to toss on another log. The third day after the most damaging ice storm in the recorded history of New Hampshire, I was over the sense of adventure and pioneer spirit that typically accompanies a loss of electricity. I'd had enough. I wanted the furnace to kick in, I wanted a long, hot bath, and I wanted a few hours of uninterrupted sleep.

"That's it," I said to my equally tired and cranky partner. "We're going to buy a generator today; I don't care how far we have to drive to find one."

It turned out we didn't have to make a long drive. Our power was restored a few hours later, making us among a very lucky few in the Monadnock region, where many people went without electricity or water for one to two weeks. Regardless, the experience had me thinking about people who came before us in these parts – people I'd spent considerable time writing about in my longtime job as an editor at the Monadnock Ledger-Transcript, where in addition to covering the local arts scene I also wrote a weekly column on local history.

The old town histories, typically written by the minister or some other prominent, educated resident, are rife with descriptions of bad weather. There was, for instance, the "Grasshopper Year" of 1826, when oppressive heat, a drought, and a surfeit of grasshoppers destroyed most of the crops and the grazing fields. There was the "Yellow Day," September 6, 1881, when the sky turned dark in the morning and did not lighten up for the rest of the day, for no apparent reason. There was the "Great Frost" of June 17, 1794, which reportedly left inch-thick ice atop rain barrels.

I've never been one to glorify those days. I expect people were mostly too hot or too cold, overworked, and miserable. But the ice storm of 2008 did point out the fact that people in said "days of olde" were better equipped to handle weather emergencies. A lot of us rural folks have well water, but without our electric pumps, we can't access the water. Same goes for oil furnaces and wood pellet stoves. They rely on the grid for power. Our battery-operated radios and flashlights work well – until the batteries run out (as those of us who searched store after store for Ds discovered).

Luckily, we learn from history. My partner and I have a generator now, wired into the household electrical system, that's ready to go should the power go out again. We have a stash of firewood and a drawer full of D batteries.

And we've got a real sense of living in historic times, weatherwise (and otherwise). So it's especially important to have a chronicle like Dave Eisenstadter's *The Weight of the Ice* to document not just the statistics but the stories of the ice storm. Dave's interviews with the people of the hardest-hit regions offer a broad and nuanced exploration of a storm that had its tragedies and frustrations, but also had moments of humor, of great generosity, and of grace. This will be a book that will be much thumbed through not just in the months following the great storm, but for generations to come.

Hancock, New Hampshire
June 19, 2009

A frozen apple tree in Norway Hill Orchard in Hancock, New Hampshire, on December 12.

Ice accumulates on a twisted vine in Guilford, Vermont.

Introduction

On an average winter morning, I wake up to the alarm of my cell phone, which I keep plugged into the wall at night. It's still dark outside, so I turn on the lights and take a hot shower. If there's time, I'll cook an omelet on my electric stove, and if there isn't, I turn down the oil heat at my apartment, get into my car, and head over to the local bagel place to get breakfast there. Then I drive to work.

For millions of people across New York State and throughout New England, every one of the things I describe was impossible on the morning of December 12, 2008, the day after one of the most devastating ice storms this region had ever experienced. Huge ice-covered branches and tree trunks had smashed down onto power lines, roads, houses, and cars. Many people were trapped in their homes, unable to get out of even their own driveways.

As frightening and disorienting as the effect of the storm itself was, it was nothing compared with the aftermath.

In some places, power outages lasted for weeks as utility workers scrambled to rebuild their entire infrastructure. Hospitals operated on emergency generator power. Fires broke out as people tried to heat their homes with wood or dilapidated generators, and houses burned unhindered with firefighters unable to negotiate the snow- and ice-covered roads. Many fled their homes looking for shelter. A few lost their lives. The security of civilization was taken away during some of the darkest, coldest weeks of the year, an interruption in a lifetime of dependence on electricity.

State emergency management departments launched enormous relief efforts. Town road crews and safety workers managed daunting cleanups. Utility companies undertook unprecedented restorations. Business owners faced challenges they'd never seen before. In the face of great adversity, New Englanders reinvented their lifestyles. Throughout the impacted area, there emerged stories of frustration and despair under the stress of learning to deal without power. There also came stories of resilience, perseverance, and community as neighbors helped one another through tough times.

When the storm hit, it was my job to get these stories as a reporter for the *Monadnock Ledger-Transcript* in Peterborough, New Hampshire. The stories poured in and for three weeks, it was most of what we reported. People were affected in unexpected and sometimes unbelievable ways, and while I felt good about our news reporting in the face of great adversities of our own, I felt this was an event that deserved something more than newspaper coverage. The huge and devastating storm was a historical event. As life gradually returned to normal, I kept making calls, driving to interviews, taking notes, and getting pictures. What resulted is this book, an attempt at capturing the story of the Ice Storm of 2008.

In putting it together, the greatest resource also became the biggest challenge: Everyone had a story. With person after person relating dramatic, touching, and unique accounts, it was hard to know when to stop. After almost every interview, I walked away with a new perspective. But at some point, one must sit down and begin to write. With the knowledge that I was leaving out literally millions of experiences, I set out to put together the best summary of the storm that I could.

There are stories and pictures in this book from New York, Massachusetts, Maine, New Hampshire, and Vermont, but the primary focus is where I live and work, the Monadnock region in southwestern New Hampshire. By all accounts, this was one of the most severely impacted regions hit by the storm, with power outages lasting the longest and devastation among the most severe.

A common cliché is that people talk about the weather when there is nothing else to talk about, but during the time of the ice storm, no subject held peoples' attention better. "Got power yet?" replaced "Hello" as the standard greeting. And as people swapped stories about the snapped trees, severed power cables, impassable roads, and their brutally disrupted lives, one villain was blamed again and again, a burden placed on trees and people alike: the weight of the ice.

My hope is that this book portrays how those affected bore that burden, and that as you look through these pages, whether you were affected or not, you can share in the experiences of those residents, business owners, relief workers, and government officials who shared them with me.

The sun rises over a frozen forest the morning of December 13 near the Taconic State Parkway between Chatham and Spencertown, New York.

BEFORE AND AFTER: *The same bushes and basketball hoop in front of Patti Hill's home in New Ipswich, New Hampshire, during the summer months (above) and days after the storm (below).*

ACT I
THE ICE STORM COMETH

A frozen tree in Portland, Maine.

Chapter 1
A Perfect Ice Storm

*"The storms of this magnitude are rare,
but they happen, and they'll happen again."*

**Hayden Frank, National Weather Service
Meteorologist, Taunton, Massachusetts**

The National Weather Service saw it coming. A high-pressure system from northern Canada was dragging cold air down to New England while a low-pressure system moved warmer air up the East Coast to the same place. In other words, it would storm, and it would be a big one.

In a Hazardous Weather Outlook released in the early morning of Monday, December 8, forecasters mentioned the potential for a "significant" winter storm. The next day, a Winter Storm Watch was issued, and by December 10, the watch was upgraded to a Winter Storm Warning and then an Ice Storm Warning. The final upgrade came mid-afternoon on Thursday, December 11 – the system was billed as a "Severe Ice Storm" that would blast through New York and New England that night. The warning to southwestern New Hampshire came from Taunton, Massachusetts. "Freezing rain will fall heavily at times with glazing easing at dawn as temperatures rise to around freezing. Heavy accumulations of glaze will probably cause power outages by midnight tonight with areas of one-inch thick ice on trees and wires, especially the east facing slopes of the Berkshires.... This is a potentially dangerous situation with long duration power outages possible, especially in the Monadnock region."

As the predictions came in, so did the school closures. Schools across New Hampshire, Massachusetts, and beyond shut down on Thursday. Utility workers stood poised to repair any damages to the lines, and emergency workers at the state level stood by. It was the typical preparation for an emergency situation.

What no one knew was just how much of an emergency the December 11 storm would become.

According to the American Meteorological Society glossary, ice storms are characterized by freezing liquid precipitation. This is caused by warm air at higher altitudes where the rain forms, and colder temperatures near the ground, where the water freezes. In these instances, the rain falling from the warm air aloft to the cold air below can become "supercooled," meaning that while it remains a liquid, its temperature is below freezing point. Supercooled drops of rain freeze instantly on contact with branches, power lines, and other exposed surfaces. This phenomenon is given the apt name

Ice damage in Berkshire County, Massachusetts.

Trees and limbs become dangerous when weighed down by more than a half an inch of ice, such as this one in Dublin, New Hampshire.

"freezing rain." Ideal conditions for such a storm involve surface temperatures far below freezing, around 20 or 25 degrees.

Although during December's storm temperatures were above that, between 29 and 32 degrees, several factors came together to produce a uniquely devastating storm. The last time such a significant storm gathered in the Northeast was in 1998, and the region it affected was further north consisting of parts of Canada and less densely populated areas of northern New York State and New England. The 2008 ice storm, however, while dropping less ice, impacted much larger populations in New Hampshire and Massachusetts.

This storm system itself was unusual, even before it began dumping ice. Beginning in the south, the system affected the lower Mississippi Valley, the Tennessee Valley, and the entire East Coast from northern Florida to Maine. In Florida and Georgia, it started at least one tornado, with thunderstorms developing from there to the Carolinas. In Pennsylvania and northern New York and New England, three to six inches of snow fell. Boston and southern New England saw between two and four inches of torrential rain. In be-

Supercooled rain encases a fence in Readsboro, Vermont.

tween, in central New England, there was between half an inch and one-and-a-half inches of ice.

"Ice storms are pretty rare," Hayden Frank of the National Weather Service in Taunton, Massachusetts, explained. "You need a certain set of ingredients. If it's too warm, you're going to get rain, and typically in the winter you're going to get snow." On December 11 and 12, Mother Nature followed the ice storm recipe exactly, which Hayden described in the storm's report – warm in the air; cold on the ground.

High temperatures in the northeast were between 55 and 60 degrees on December 10, a balmy day for that time of year. Winds from the south continued to blow the warm air into the northeast, and during the ice storm, between 5,000 and 15,000 feet in elevation, warm air allowed rain to form. While New England was enjoying a fair day on the 10th, southeastern Canada experienced temperatures in the teens. As the winds from the south blew warmer air aloft, winds coming from the northeast blew colder, heavier air down from Canada, until in the early morning hours of December 11, surface temperatures in central New England hovered around freezing.

All of this would have been little trouble had the storm been confined to daylight hours. During the day on December 11, the sun kept temperatures high enough for the falling precipitation to remain liquid upon impact. The trouble started as the sun set and the temperature dropped. The Weather Service recorded temperatures between 29 and 32 degrees at ground level, allowing ice to accumulate through the night.

The icing on the cake, as it were, was the fact that a low-pressure system formed in the coastal area of southeastern Massachusetts during the early morning hours of December 12, when the ice storm was at its peak. This weather system ensured a steady rush of wind from the north, meaning that the inflow of cold Canadian air persisted through the night instead of eroding as the rain fell.

According to Taunton meteorologist Joe Dellicarpini, who worked with Hayden to create the weather report for the December storm, a quarter inch of accumulated ice is the point at which branches start to bend. Half an inch is when they start to break, bringing down nearby wires as they go.

The area that accrued more than half an inch of ice stretched across New York and New England. In a situation in which every degree counts, strange patterns emerged based on wind direction and elevations. In the Monadnock region, Keene, which sits in a valley, experienced few outages and a low amount of ice accumulation. The surrounding towns of Chesterfield, Harrisville, Dublin, Jaffrey, Fitzwilliam, and Rindge were all heavily impacted. Just 30 miles away, New Ipswich, New Hampshire, wound up being one of the hardest hit towns in the storm. In some areas, more than an inch-and-a-half of ice built up, snapping trees and utility poles in half.

Huddled in their homes, the people that lived in the affected areas crouched in terror as the weather had its say, pounding tree limbs and wires onto the ground. From New York to Maine, they lay awake listening to the overture of what was to follow.

Fallen trees litter Carol Kender-McNiff's property in Rutland, Massachusetts, on December 12.

Chapter 2
POP... CRACK... BOOM!

"It was 1:15 Friday morning when all the trees were exploding out back. It sounded like cannon fire or gunshots."

**Andrew Freeman, owner of Dublin General Store,
Dublin, New Hampshire**

Rebecca Karam was 37 weeks pregnant on the morning of December 12 when she woke up to a loud "bang." A transformer next to her home in Ashby, Massachusetts, blew up at 1 in the morning, and she realized immediately the house was without power. She and her husband lay awake for the rest of the night as trees snapped and came down all around them. "That one was really big…. That one was really big," they repeated to one another, hoping the next branch wouldn't be the one that came through the roof.

Frightening as it sounds, their experience was typical all across the Northeast. People were jerked awake that night by the sounds of splitting limbs and the flashes of bursting transformers lighting up the sky. Many described it as being in a war zone with bombs blasting. As the violent noises awakened more and more people, they found their clocks frozen and nightlights extinguished, confirming what many suspected – the power was out.

Meanwhile, ice clung to tree limbs and power lines, building up from a quarter-inch to a half-inch and then nearly an inch thick in

This tree leaning against Pam Crook's Greenfield, New Hampshire, house broke through the screen of the sliding door leading to her bedroom, but stopped just short of the glass.

some locations. In Lyndeborough, New Hampshire, Chris Pfeil had great cause to be concerned. He is a maple syrup producer, and many of the snapping trees he heard were the ones he depended on for a living. With a partner, he has a business called "The Maple Guys," which distributes maple syrup as far abroad as Japan. At 2:30 in the morning, Chris could do nothing to protect his orchard. He stood outside his house listening to the sounds in the darkness.

Further east, in Kingston, New Hampshire, Glenn Coppelman sat awake with other maple trees on his mind… the huge, 100-year-old silver maples standing right next to his home. Keeping vigil on the first floor of his house, he was fearful one would come through the roof. As limbs fell they hit branches on other trees as they came down. He heard the cracks above and felt the vibrations below as the limbs pelted the ground.

For all the darkness that would come later, many described this night's darkness as the scariest. Unable to see his orchard trees, Chris was free to imagine a total loss. Glenn's worry was that his own house was being assailed by an unseen army of branches. As for Rebecca, her husband, and their unborn child, they were together, but did not know if they were safe.

In those early morning hours, people invented their own mythology to describe the experience. Kenyon Acton, a student at Marlboro College in Marlboro, Vermont, said the falling trees sounded like a giant monster with a club. In Nelson, New Hampshire, Elice Laughner said the wind in the trees sounded like rattling bones. Having grabbed her daughter from the treacherous top floor of her house where branches were breaking on the roof, Liz Hardison from Jaffrey, New Hampshire, said the sound was like a dinosaur running through the woods, knocking down all the trees. "CRACK, BANG! CRACK, BANG!" she said, animatedly describing the noise.

No one knew when or if a tree would come crashing through the house. For John Matesowicz in Gardner, Massachusetts, the night got worse and worse. "My kids kept waking up screaming," John said, the horror of the experience fresh in his voice even though more than a month had passed by the time we spoke. "We were all huddled up in bed. It was one of the creepiest things I have experienced in my whole life." At 10:30 p.m., John saw a flash of blue that lit up the sky, followed by a sea of blackness. A transformer had blown. Every 10 or 15 seconds, another tree in his neighborhood would fall, many hitting neighbors' houses and a few landing against his own house. One fell directly on his car, caving in the entire hood. As it turned out, the engine still ran and John was able to drive it the next day, after cutting up the tree on top of it.

Cars are one thing, but the inner sanctum of the bedroom is another. At Pam Crook's house in Greenfield, New Hampshire, she described what she heard as "crash!" "boom!" "bang!" all night long. Among the hundreds of trees she estimates came down on her property was one that almost wound up sleeping next to her. "One tree came down and landed against the bedroom," Pam said. "We have a sliding glass door, and it came through the screen and stopped short of the glass."

Beneta Hadley of Jaffrey may have had the rudest awakening of all. In an essay she wrote about her storm experience published in the *Ledger-Transcript*, she described how a tree broke through her roof right above her. "One of the branches stopped about two inches beside my head," Beneta wrote. "The ice cold rain came pouring in and gave me an ice cold shower."

The night was long for many, but the sun eventually rose in the morning, dispelling the hidden terrors but revealing overwhelming devastation. It was time for the people of the Northeast to get out and do what they could. Chris Pfeil pushed the thoughts of his maple trees aside and went to get gas for his generator. Rebecca Karam's husband bid his pregnant wife farewell as he prepared to head into work.

Even a sign in Sullivan, New Hampshire, takes on an icy splendor.

ACT II
A REGION TRANSFORMED

Trees lean and limbs hang over the access road to Monadnock State Park in Jaffrey, New Hampshire.

Chapter 3
First Glimpses

"Every single power line was down in the middle of the ground. None of the roads were passable. Every street corner you turned looked like a war scene, a frozen hurricane."

John Matesowicz, Gardner, Massachusetts

In Maine, more than 230,000 households awoke Friday morning without power – 30 percent of the state. The number was 300,000 in New York and 350,000 in Massachusetts. The hardest hit state was New Hampshire, with 420,000 households without power – more than half of its residents. Add in 40,000 who lost power in Vermont, and the grand total is 1,340,000 homes without power. Multiply that number by an average of 2.7 people per household, and a good estimate of the number of people without power becomes 3,618,000. More than three and a half million people were without power in the northeastern United States on December 12, 2008.

And the blackouts were only the first part of the story. Those venturing outside found damaged property along with a shower of broken branches and ice scattered treacherously on roads and driveways. And still, trees continued to fall.

The Ice Storm of 2008, as it became known, dumped ice onto the two southernmost counties in Vermont, seven southern and

Downed trees and power lines in Londonderry, New Hampshire, on December 13.

coastal counties in Maine, 16 counties in eastern central New York, and seven counties in western, central, and northeastern Massachusetts. In New Hampshire, the ice covered nearly the entire state except for the sparsely populated northern tip.

In Stoddard, New Hampshire, Chris Young was frightened the morning she woke up without power. Her cordless telephone did not work, and neither did anything else in her house. Her employers were able to reach her on a phone that plugged into the wall, telling her work was canceled for the day because no one had power. Chris and her fiancé decided to have a look for themselves. "We went outside literally into devastation," she said. "A giant limb that went down off of a birch tree had missed my car by a foot. Moving around, you could hear sounds like glass breaking. Trees were tumbling and splitting off from all angles."

Oscar and Patti Hills in New Ipswich, New Hampshire, had their own near miss. The family's new truck was sitting in the driveway and three feet above it, suspended on a wire that had not yet broken, was a tree trunk. Their son quickly moved the truck.

Across the state in Durham, home of the University of New Hampshire's main campus, Jan Heirtzler spent the night with her three children, aged 8, 5, and 11 months, camped out in her oldest child's room, away from a large pine tree on the other side of the house. At 6 a.m. Friday, a tree overhanging the driveway began to drop branches, several of which knocked out their power, phone, and cable lines, and one of which landed directly on top of her car, crushing it. Jan called her husband, who was coming in from the airport that morning, and told him to get a rental car. Schools were closed, so everyone stayed home, waiting for the power to return – a wait they would find lasted quite a while.

Daybreak did not mean the end of the destruction for everyone. Jennifer Lund in Argyle, Maine, awoke to find a section of the fence surrounding her chicken coop crushed by a toppled tree. Thinking it was safe to let the chickens out anyway, Jennifer opened the coop and proceeded to repair the section of fence. With weakened limbs still falling in the morning breeze, this turned out to be a bad idea. The wind picked up and a branch snapped off of a nearby tree squashing another section of the fence, and freeing the chickens. "I had to chase them around the yard," Jennifer said.

Urban areas were affected as well as rural ones. In Worcester, Massachusetts, Victor Monahan drove with his video camera recording the aftermath of the storm and posted the results on YouTube under the name RazKazProductions. The video shows downed

A street in Worcester, Massachusetts, is completely covered with fallen debris on December 12.

A neighborhood filled with ice in Portland, Maine.

branches and wires lining the sidewalks and spilling out onto the streets. Enormous pools of water surround cars. All over, people are in their yards, attempting to clear away the debris with their hands and with chain saws. The video ends with the understated text, "It was pretty bad."

In the city of Nashua, New Hampshire, Kent Koeninger thought he would be able to find a cup of coffee and a working Internet connection somewhere the day after the storm, but this was no easy feat. The Panera Bread near his house was without power. The Starbucks was up and running, but it was crowded to the gills with people who had the same idea. Signs of the devastation were present throughout the city, but some of the roads were clear by the next morning. "Some traffic lights were on and some were off," Kent said. "Lots of branches fell in the roads, but you could actually drive. It wasn't very icy."

On his way to work in Boston Friday morning, Matt Cohen had to leave Nashua by Route 111A. Bent trees loomed threateningly over the state road, and Matt had to zigzag around fallen limbs. "There were two points at which there were downed wires in the streets, and I was questioning what I was doing going in to work," he said. "But the car ahead of me drove over them, so they were apparently safe enough to drive over." He added that, miraculously, he arrived at work on time.

Ice brings down trees in Altamont, New York, the day after the storm.

Mount Washington, New England's tallest peak and supposedly the site of the worst weather in the Northeast, was nonetheless spared the brunt of the storm. Mount Washington Observatory meteorologist Peter Crane said he saw ice form 10 or 15 miles away, but not at the summit.

The Monadnock region's centerpiece, Mount Monadnock, fared far worse. The entirety of Monadnock State Park closed down because of the branches that fell among its miles of trails. Normally, Mount Monadnock is considered the second most climbed mountain in the world after Japan's Mount Fuji, with cross-country skiing and snowshoeing continuing through the winter. But the ice stopped all activity on the mountain in its tracks. "The damage there was pretty extensive," New Hampshire Forest Society member Geoff Jones said of Monadnock. "The young generation of hardwoods were all snapped off and bent over. It looked like somebody dropped a bomb in there." The eastern side of the mountain was hit the hardest, and the greatest damage was below 2,500 feet in elevation on the 3,165-foot peak.

Across the Connecticut River, in Marlboro, Vermont, finals were canceled at Marlboro College, as the whole area was covered in ice. Stuck on campus and waiting to be evacuated, Kenyon Acton joined a group of students playing basketball to pass the time. The hoop was frozen, and as soon as someone sank the first basket, the ball was stuck, suspended in the air, waiting for the ice to thaw.

Described above were first impressions of the storm observed from front doorways and during early morning hours. As shocking as it was for people to see their cars smashed and yards littered with debris, it was when they tried to leave home that the horror of the ice storm truly took hold. For many, the New England adage "You can't get there from here" was an inescapable reality.

Nothing but net… at least until the ice melts. Taken three days after the storm, this photo shows the result of an extremely quick game of basketball at Marlboro College in Marlboro, Vermont.

A car swerves around a fallen branch the day after the storm in Peterborough, New Hampshire.

Chapter 4
You Can't Get There From Here

"There was a guy flashing his lights at me and I didn't know what was going on until I saw a tree in the middle of the road."

Norm Sturgeon, Lempster, New Hampshire

Jeff Petrovitch woke up for work at 3 a.m. on Friday, December 12. A cab driver with Adventure Taxi Service in Keene, New Hampshire, Jeff got ready for his usual Friday shift of 4 a.m. to noon. One look out the window, however, was enough to tell him this would be anything but an ordinary Friday.

Jeff did not own a car, relying instead on an Aprilia scooter to take him the five miles between his house in Swanzey and the cab service in neighboring Keene. That Friday, Jeff decided to call in a cab for himself. Another driver at the end of his shift picked him up and passed on an assignment, a woman at a Keene hospital who needed to get to her home in Jaffrey. "She was there since eight at night," Jeff said of the woman. "No one would drive her. She was happy that we finally said we would try it."

While Keene and Swanzey for the most part avoided the devastation of the ice storm, Jaffrey was one of the towns hardest hit. On his first fare of the day, Jeff found himself traveling into the heart of the devastation. Driving south on Route 12 toward the outskirts of Jaffrey, he soon encountered downed trees and utility poles. Afraid

An ice-covered tree blocks half the road in Dublin, New Hampshire.

cables lying across the road could be live, he waited until he saw another car drive over them before making the attempt himself.

"No one has power; I turn left and Mr. Mike's [gas station] has no power," Jeff said. "Down the road there is a plow truck stopped and I think, 'What is going on here!' I proceed to try to drive around it, and just as I'm passing it down the hill, there is a tree completely blocking Route 119. I think, 'Well, can't go this way,' and I swing the taxi around."

Trying alternate routes, Jeff found all roads toward Jaffrey either partially or fully blocked by trees. Some scraped the top of his car while others hit the sides. Jeff said he drove over a small tree and got out to push another out of the way. The longer it took, the more antsy his passenger became. "She's yakking nonstop and I'm pretty scared," Jeff said. "This is not my car; this is a company vehicle. I'm just trying to keep the taxi on the road."

After nearly three hours driving around and finding the way blocked, Jeff returned to Keene and dropped his passenger off at a Dunkin Donuts. At 9 a.m., two-and-a-half hours later, he returned to pick her up and try again. By that time, the major roads were clear enough to allow him to pass, but the best he could do was drop her off at the base of her driveway. "I can't get up her hill because a huge tree is blocking it," Jeff said. "So she had to walk up her hill."

Across the state, at the same time, David Hayes of Nashua was trying to approach the Monadnock region from the opposite direction. I spoke with him days after the storm and his story was published in the *Ledger-Transcript*. David, a food production manager for Sodexo Food Service at Monadnock Community Hospital in Peterborough, spent seven hours on the roads between his house and the hospital, normally just over an hour commute. Setting out at 4 in the morning, David negotiated his way around road blocks and the trees that continued to fall. "I thought, 'I can't turn around; I have patients to feed,'" he said. "My boss was home ill; I knew she wasn't going to come in."

From Nashua to Milford, New Hampshire, David experienced few problems. The troubles started when he crossed into the Monadnock region. Almost immediately upon entering Wilton, New Hampshire, he was stopped at a roadblock along with several other cars. Teaming up with three other cars, David and his small caravan

The morning after the ice storm, this smashed tree blocks the way in Merrimack, New Hampshire.

A dirt road in Dublin, New Hampshire, flanked on both sides by leaning, ice-covered trees.

found a side road they thought would bypass the roadblock. But turning off the main road while trees were falling turned out to be a huge mistake. Trees fell in front and behind, trapping the cars. One even fell on the cab of a pickup that was with them, but luckily the driver was not injured. Although he had done military service in Kuwait, David admitted he had never been as scared in his life as

A tree leans over power lines on Route 101 on Temple Mountain in New Hampshire near the Peterborough/Temple line.

when he was trapped on that road. "We were there for two hours just hanging there, not knowing what was going on," David said. "I didn't even know these people, but things happen and you just pull together."

A man who lived on the road came out with a chain saw to help, and the four cars backed out to the main road, sheepishly returning to the roadblock, where they were eventually let through. Farther down the road, a second roadblock halted them again, right before they came into Peterborough. "I started crying, 'This is bullsh-t! We've come this far!'" he said.

Helping road workers clear the way, David spent two more hours dragging debris from the road until a man next to him was whipped in the face by a branch and began bleeding from a three-and-a-half inch gash. By then, a small passage had been cleared, and David and the other man were allowed to drive to the hospital. "I never thought it was going to be as bad as it was," he said. "You take these side roads and it's almost like sniper fire. But we got there."

In Peterborough, the police and fire chiefs pulled their people off the roads until daylight hours, citing the dangerous situation. Trees were breaking, and the town workers could hear them, but not see them go down. In the early morning hours, town officials had de-

A Sullivan, New Hampshire, resident looks at a birch tree hanging across the road.

clared a state of emergency, and when the sun came up, they assessed the damage. "It was very clear very quickly that every road in town was impacted," Public Works Director Rodney Bartlett said. "Obviously some were worse than others, but every road had some level of damage from broken trees and downed wires."

The major damage extended across five states. In New Hampshire, 400 local roads and 150 segments of state roads were blocked. The New York Department of Transportation deployed 1,200 workers and 750 pieces of heavy equipment to clear the roads. Officials from Maine reported hundreds of road closures, and many were blocked in Vermont as well. In Massachusetts, thousands of roads were impacted, among them sections of Route 2, which, apart from Interstate 90, is one of the main arterial routes across the state.

Bruce Griffin, of Amherst, Massachusetts, had an important reason to venture out on the roads. While he had not lost power, his father, George, of Haverhill, Massachusetts, had. George was 90 and unsteady on his feet, but Bruce had to convince him over the phone that evacuating the house was a good idea. "He didn't want me to go to the trouble of going out there," Bruce said. "He thought he'd be fine if he'd just stay in bed."

Taking the shortest route, the trip would have been just shy of 100 miles, but Bruce had to take the long way around, heading south to the Massachusetts Turnpike to eventually get to the extreme northeast part of the state. When he arrived in Haverhill, it was dark again, and power had not been restored. "The only lights you'd see for the most part were the headlights of cars and lights where people had generators," Bruce said.

When he reached his father's street, he found it blocked at both ends. Driving around a fire truck and then around a road barrier, he managed to get to his father's driveway, where a branch was partially blocking the way. After a final bit of convincing in person, Bruce got his father into the car, turned around, and headed back across the state. "It was an adventure," he said. "On the way back I took Route 2 hoping that 202 would be open by then, but I had to go all the way west through Millers Falls, [Massachusetts]. It was dark and my father was praising me for my resourcefulness. I enjoyed that."

Preferring to stay rather than have his son come get him, George had his own way of looking at the situation. "I wasn't thrilled with the idea of moving out for a day or two," he said. "Being 90 years old, I'm kind of used to it by now, catastrophes like that. There was the hurricane years back, big storms, snow or rain. You continue living; that's all." Still, George admitted he had seen many storms, but nothing to the extent of the 2008 storm. He has lived in Massachusetts his whole life.

George had not been to his son's house in a few years, and Bruce said it was nice having him there for a while. By Sunday, power had been restored to Haverhill, and father and son took to the road again. This time, rather than driving through devastation, they drove through the beauty of sparkling ice in the sun on roads that had finally been cleared.

Clearing the roads was a Herculean effort and just one of the many tasks the storm imposed on the people in the area it devastated. From the rescue workers to utility workers to those just working to clear their own way out, one thing remained constant: work, and lots of it.

A Worcester, Massachusetts, resident gathers branches from the front yard as a tree service worker clips branches from above.

Chapter 5
Workers of the World Un-Ice

*"Our president drove to school when the power went out;
she got in her car and made breakfast with a bunch of students."*

**Kenyon Acton, Student, Marlboro College,
Marlboro, Vermont**

Like the trunk-snapping weight put on the trees, the ice storm placed a burden on people's shoulders to manage the cleanup effort and other developing emergencies. Mostly unwashed and unshaven, and with miles of dangerous road ahead of them, those without power assessed what needed to be done. It was time to get to work.

Neal Cass, the town administrator for Antrim, New Hampshire, lost power at his house in nearby Hancock, New Hampshire, Thursday night, but made the assumption it would be back on soon. Driving the branch-covered roads and arriving to work the next morning to discover the entire town was without power, a different reality dawned on him. This was a true disaster. Neal and other town officials had their first emergency management meeting early that afternoon.

Immediately, Antrim's emergency management team decided to open an emergency command center and a shelter in the upstairs

(above and on opposite page) Brent Boeckmann takes a chainsaw to a tree that landed in his yard in Dublin, New Hampshire, clearing the way to his garage.

of the town office building. Sending a town bus to a nearby retirement community, they collected 10 residents from their homes and brought them downtown. Almost immediately, volunteers began coming through the doors to cook meals and set up cots that had been provided by the Red Cross.

Neal had been a town manager and a selectman before that, but he had been hired in Antrim only a few months earlier. Spending his nights at the town offices in the days following the storm, he joked that he didn't know he had signed up for a live-in position. "We were awake all night just to monitor everything that was going on," he said. "The next night, things had quieted down somewhat, and I slept really well on my office floor."

While Neal and other town officials staffed command centers, town police, road crews, and volunteer firefighters bore the brunt of relief work out in the streets. Firefighters in particular made up the backbone of such efforts, performing residence checks, helping citizens, and cutting open roads in addition to responding to calls to fight fires.

Steve Weber, a firefighter both for Dublin, New Hampshire, and neighboring Harrisville, focused on his hometown of Harrisville during the ice storm. After waiting for his wife to get home from a trip the day after the storm to take care of their 8-year-old son, Steve got to work sawing trees from the roads and supervising younger workers and volunteers doing the same. The trees were heavily weighed down from the immense amount of ice frozen to their branches, and Steve said he thought one might easily snap back and crack someone across the skull. Luckily, this did not happen. "It was scary; those trees were loaded," Steve said. "There was a lot of danger, and I did not like going out there."

When the roads were relatively clear, he and other firefighters drove around in the fire trucks, checking on residents and responding to emergency medical calls. They knocked on doors, made sure people knew about the local shelters, and asked if they needed anything. If someone's basement was flooded, they pumped it out. If someone needed food or water, firefighters did their best to find supplies. Anything that needed to be done, volunteer firefighters

A horse enclosed in an icy fence in Rutland, Massachusetts, on December 12.

were ready to lend a hand. Their goal was to reach every house in Harrisville, and they kept at it until they achieved it.

There were no fire calls in Harrisville, but the Temple, New Hampshire, Fire Department had two that they couldn't reach because of impassable roads. One was a vehicle fire in which a truck was charred. The other, a structure fire, gutted a house on Mansfield Road.

Phil Schlictling of Spofford, New Hampshire, lost a part of his house to a fire on December 16, which he suspects began from a spark from a generator. By that time, the roads were cleared, but the two-alarm fire still consumed the kitchen and two bathrooms before it was extinguished. Through the night, 50 firefighters fought off the blaze. Phil decided to salvage the remainder of the house, later replacing the section the fire had destroyed.

In addition to those who lost property, a few lost their lives. Among calls for downed wires and minor medical calls, Francestown, New Hampshire, Fire Chief Larry Kullgren and his department were called to the house of an 84-year-old man by a neighbor. The man had collapsed while trying to operate his woodstove and was incoherent when firefighters arrived with medical personnel. They rushed him to Monadnock Community Hospital, but he later died there.

New Ipswich, as stated earlier, was named by some as the town hardest hit by the ice storm. The top of seemingly every tree snapped off, leaving branches strewn all over the roads and exposing raw wood on trunks as far as the eye could see. Oak trees two feet in diameter snapped like twigs, along with hundreds of utility

A frozen backyard in Wells, Maine.

In Nelson, New Hampshire, Lisa Sieverts stands behind a toppled trunk leaning on a car.

poles. For Police Lieutenant Tim Carpenter, it was the most widespread damage he had ever seen.

For New Ipswich, as with other towns, the main goals were to establish an emergency command center, to clear the roads, and to check on all residents. Police, firefighters, and other workers were grouped into teams and assigned zones within the town. The teams checked every house and every road. "The biggest problem is you can't train for that type of thing," said Police Chief Garrett Chamberlain. "You can't practice or do a drill to that level. You couldn't even set it up to be realistic. What happened was we dealt with something that encompassed the entire town, all 33 square miles. There wasn't a specific area we could isolate and quarantine."

At the Red Cross in Nashua, New Hampshire, 25-year-old Ashley Pushkarewicz had become one of the youngest Red Cross emergency management directors in the region about a month before the ice storm. Ashley described the experience as "trial by fire and ice." In the first week, there was an extremely large fire in the city of Nashua, and the ice storm followed a few weeks later.

When emergencies are expected, the Red Cross puts specific volunteers on alert, and the rest are free unless they are activated. Ashley, an Antrim resident, was expecting to call it a night the evening of December 11, but the phone rang around 12:30 in the morning. "A duplex of 12 individuals had a tree go through it," Ashley said. "I hung up the phone, and then got another phone call that a se-

Fallen trees surround the welcome sign into Peterborough, New Hampshire.

Icy covered trees (above) loom in Harrisville, New Hampshire. The damage at Monadnock State Park (right) was extensive and took months to repair.

Work gloves on and chainsaw at the ready, workers set about clearing the road in Londonderry, New Hampshire, on December 13.

nior center was down [without power] with 50 individuals. At that point, I thought I needed to get in the car and go to Nashua. That was right when the power went off where I was living."

The Nashua Red Cross serves 16 New Hampshire towns in addition to the city of Nashua: Amherst, Brookline, Greenville, Hollis, Hudson, Lyndeborough, Mason, Merrimack, Milford, Mont Vernon, New Ipswich, Pelham, Salem, Temple, Wilton, and Windham. Located in the south central portion of the state, these towns were some of the worst hit by the ice storm.

By 8 in the morning on December 12, Ashley had contacted all of the emergency management directors in those towns, and worked on finding out where the most damage was, coordinating where shelters would open, and figuring out how to get supplies such as cots, blankets, and bottled water to the shelters. Everything Ashley and other emergency management directors did was fed into databases at the state Emergency Operations Center in Concord, the state capital. "Picture a big NASA space center with big screens everywhere," Ashley said of the EOC.

While Ashley fielded hundreds of calls, the most memorable came when one of the volunteers called in a "death," which wound up being a pet fish. "It was one of those funny moments," Ashley said. "It was during a snowstorm and one of them said, 'You need to come here right away. We had a death.' They would not explain to me what was going on. They were devastated, and told me they performed CPR on the fish. At that point, I might have burst out laughing."

The Red Cross does not accept animals in its shelters, but in the shelters in Ashley's coverage area, the organization partnered with the New Hampshire Disaster Animal Response Team, which helped house pets. According to the Pets Act, signed into law in

Route 101 near Temple Mountain in Temple, New Hampshire, is down to one lane as workers move trees and restore wires.

Firefighters assess ice damage in Sullivan, New Hampshire.

2006, states are required to have considerations for pets in disaster situations in order to receive federal aid, which was one of the primary things NH DART was in the process of addressing during the storm, according to founder and executive director Lora DePlante from New Ipswich.

At the local level, neighbors organized their own individual responses, using chainsaws to free vehicles and open driveways. Paul Landry of New Ipswich worked as a sawyer for hire, clearing brush out of driveways. Sullivan, New Hampshire, resident Don Primrose hacked through his driveway, then used his plow to clear roads for others near his house. In Heath, Massachusetts, Don Freeman was lucky to have a neighbor clear out his driveway because he was worried he would be too accident-prone using a chain saw himself.

Laura Gingras, vice president of philanthropy and community relations at Monadnock Community Hospital, walked the two miles between her house and the hospital to get to work the morning after the ice storm. The roads were not passable by car. Trees and branches were still falling around her, but she managed to get into work unscathed. When she arrived, the hospital was on generator power, a situation that lasted for four days as crews worked to get the area back online. Meeting with other members of the executive team, Laura discussed what needed to be done, with a particular eye toward staffing. Not everyone had the ability to walk to work. "We had staff that had been on all night and staff who were slated to relieve them who couldn't get in," Laura said. "We were trying to reach whoever we could who could come in."

Many with ice storm-related problems looked to the hospital, not knowing where else to turn. The hospital received calls from community members and from town officials trying to coordinate relief efforts. People came into the emergency room just looking for warmth or a cup of coffee. Elective surgery dangerous to perform on generator power was canceled, and all efforts were diverted to the ER. Everything was done with the hospital understaffed, and while the hospital itself stayed open, four satellite practices in Antrim, Jaffrey, Rindge, and New Ipswich were shut down the day after the storm.

Reporting for the *Ledger-Transcript*, I spoke with Dr. Eric Lasky a week-and-a-half into the aftermath. For a few hours, he was the only doctor in the entire hospital, arriving only 15 minutes late to work Friday morning after moving a downed telephone wire by hand and having a neighbor chainsaw him out of his road. "I think we had a dozen ambulances in the first three or four hours," he said. "They were just dumping patient after patient in there. Every bed was filled, and there were people in the halls."

Road workers in Readsboro, Vermont.

Different patterns emerged as new patients came in. At first, they saw three people who were struck by tree branches. Then there was a wave of elderly residents without heat who came in looking for a warm place to stay. Many of them had requirements like oxygen that had to be plugged in. Days later, carbon monoxide poisoning from improperly installed generators proved to be an issue.

Eric worked a 12-hour shift five out of the first six days after the storm, and every shift was incredibly busy. The Peterborough shelter at South Meadow School, the local middle school, opened during the second day of the aftermath, and many who had taken refuge in the hospital were diverted there. But even during those first days, patients took things in stride. "In spite of the chaos and how busy it was, it was amazing that from the patients who had to wait, you never heard a single complaint," Eric said. "They were grateful we and they were there. It was really nice." Eric and others described their resilience in the face of the storm as being in "survival mode." There was work to be done, and no one could afford to burn out. His own home was out for 10 days, and at the time I spoke with him, he had just had his power restored. What impressed him was the sustained effort of those working to restore the downed lines (see Chapter 16).

People looking for supplies came to depend on nearby shops, and those stores opened their doors as early as they could. Dublin General Store owner Andrew Freeman opened at 1:30 in the morning on December 12, minutes after power had been knocked out. Police and state road crews were already on the road, and some stopped in for coffee. The store's chef, Davida Rondeau, made food using a grill in back of the store, and Dublin residents were able to stop in for supplies. In Antrim, Rick Edmunds opened Edmunds' Hardware Store, which has been in his family for four generations. Using flashlights to guide customers around the store, Rick and his staff quickly sold out of gas cans, flashlights, and batteries. The Holiday Inn in Keene had 35 of its 80 rooms available Friday morning at 7 a.m.; a few hours later, they had sold out.

At the U.S. Post Office in Peterborough, with or without power, supervisor of customer services and delivery Dave Poirier had a statement carved into the James Farley Post Office in New York City to live up to: "Neither snow nor rain nor heat nor gloom of night stays these couriers from the swift completion of their appointed rounds." With no lights and no heat, the staff sorted mail under flashlights and battery operated lanterns, three of which

Dave brought in himself. The steel covering of the service window could only be opened electronically, and all of the office's scales were electronic, so customer service was reduced to selling stamps. Rural carriers made their best attempts to make deliveries, but roads were closed and some deliveries were delayed. Eventually, however, everything got through. "We deliver under the most adverse conditions," Dave said. "There were roads that were impassable, bridges were out, but we could always go around and deliver the mail. We made alternate plans to get it through."

In the office, Bonnie Pomasko worked at sorting mail with inside temperatures in the 50s. Her hands started to get numb, but she and other sorters got it done every day for the five days the post office lacked power. In her 30 years with the post office, which included other disasters such as floods, she said she had never experienced anything like what happened after the ice storm.

While many businesses stayed open or went into overdrive to accommodate those without power, schools closed across the Northeast. In the Peterborough area, school districts were closed through winter break, giving students a vacation from December 11 to January 5. Although facility coordinators worked to keep the buildings warm and functional, students stayed home.

Several institutions of higher learning, including Franklin Pierce University in Rindge, New Hampshire, and Marlboro College in Marlboro, Vermont, canceled their finals. The campuses were evacuated, and everyone who was able to leave for home was encouraged to do so. Academic work was put on hold so that the more immediate work, staying warm and staying safe, could take place. Eventually, the ice storm turned to rain, the rain stopped, the tree limbs stopped falling, and the sun came out from behind the fading clouds. Those working ceaselessly to restore power, clean up their property, or keep people safe looked up and had to admit one thing: When the light hit the ice-covered trees just right, it was truly beautiful.

The moon shines through icy branches in Nelson, New Hampshire.

Chapter 6
A Forest of Crystal

---

*"It was beautiful. Every single branch was covered
with ice. It was like a forest of crystal."*

Henry Bley-Vroman, Alstead, New Hampshire

Cities like New York and Las Vegas flaunt lights of every color imaginable at all hours of the night. Blues, reds, and greens flash above streets filled with the red and white lights of cars cruising through blinking yellow traffic lights. In rainforests and other tropics, bright birds and flowers light up the scenery. Usually limited to white on the ground, grey in the sky, and bare, brown trees in between, wintry New England had something to rival those displays when the sun came out following the ice storm.

Kendra McGhee works as the assistant manager for the exhibition gallery of the celebrated Sharon Arts Center in Peterborough. A photographer, she always carries a camera so she can take a picture whenever she is inspired. From the minute she looked out the window the first morning after the storm, she knew she had found a big subject. Blades of grass covered with ice outside her door were each as thick as her pinky. Branches above seemed to be covered with glass. A native of California, Kendra had never seen so much ice. "It was absolutely gorgeous," she said. "I had a lot of fun travel-

A dog explores his icy yard in Rutland, Massachusetts, the day after the storm.

ing around taking photographs and taking it all in. It was a visual treat although experientially it wasn't always wonderful."

Awestruck, Kendra took shots of dried up weeds whose coating of ice magnified their details in beautiful ways. Usually preferring to take close-ups, she now photographed sweeping landscapes. When the sun came out, it glistened off the ice-covered trees, and light reflected through the bent branches. They twinkled, displaying brilliant colors. "All of a sudden, everything that is normal and not lovely was just extraordinary, even down to a single blade of grass or a garbage can or a chain link fence," she said.

The gruesome was among the spectacular. Among the first sights

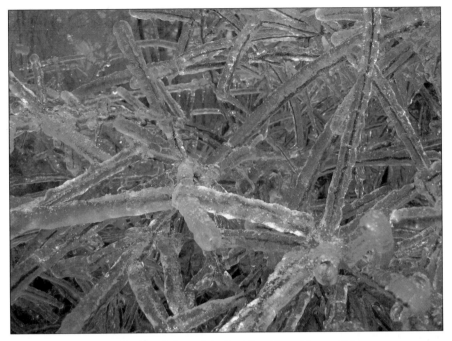

Branches encased in ice (above) in Dublin, New Hampshire.
The setting sun (below) reflects off the ice on Pinnacle Mountain in Lyndeborough, New Hampshire, the day after the storm.

Ice-covered buds and berries (above) and pine needles (below) in Portland, Maine.

The view (above) from Ann Stokes Loop Hiking Trail at Madame Sherri Forest in West Chesterfield, New Hampshire, on December 14. Frozen spruce (below) in Readsboro, Vermont.

The view of Mount Monadnock from Sullivan, New Hampshire, on the morning of December 13.

awaiting Kendra when she left her apartment was the source of a loud boom she had heard the previous night, a large tree lying across three cars at the house next door. Confronting such images filled her with a sense of adventure, and she set off on a drive with her fiancé through the devastated streets, her camera in hand.

Kendra's experience was far from unique. Photographer Michael Miller of Harrisville said the best day to go out was the Sunday after the storm. Traveling with his wife, and ripping a tire open driving over rough terrain, Michael shot and assembled a series of postcards with images taken from the ice. "Everything out there was crystallized," Michael said. "The beauty of it was outstanding." The postcards were successful. Michael sold a lot of them, and an art professor at nearby Keene State College tracked him down because of them.

Debbie Lindsay from Hubbardston, Massachusetts, enjoyed the ice in the sunshine as well. Her husband Allen assessed the roads as a "nightmare," but the roads were not in her thoughts. "I wasn't looking at the hours of cleanup," Debbie said. "I was looking at the sun and the glistening of the ice. It stayed for weeks after."

Over in Hollis, Maine, Leigh Libby fixed an ice-damaged fence, but also took time to take in the beauty of the morning. That night, driving home after dark in the near-full moon, Leigh turned off her lights and watched the moon shine through the trees. "The tree tops were just sparkling and it made me think of the magic of Narnia," she said. "Every branch on every tree was just sparkling, and it was a privilege to be a part of it."

Back in the Monadnock region, improvising a route home to avoid closed roads, Kendra and her fiancé looked up at the moon through the ice-coated trees. Kendra noted the subtle beauty of the moonlit glassy figures that formed among the twigs that would have been impossible to see in the darkness.

Max Nunnemaker stood in the moonlight in Nelson with his girlfriend, Lisa Sieverts. He had a camera, but he didn't think it was doing him much good. "You had the sense that there was no way you could capture it in a photograph," Max said. "You just had to stand outside and stare for an hour because it was so amazingly beautiful."

Photographers for the *Ledger-Transcript* captured whatever they could. The newsroom had photos of devastated roads, children clearing brush, and people temporarily displaced from their homes, but there were photos of the forest of crystal as well. Editor Dave Anderson, like many in the region, drove to the apple orchard at the top of Norway Hill in his hometown of Hancock. Through the glittering apple trees, there was a clear view of Mount Monadnock covered with ice. The orchard's owner, Peg McLeod, told Dave that people with cameras were coming and going all day.

In January, the newspaper held a competition for the best ice storm photo, with Kendra as one of the jury members. Among the winners was a photo taken at McLeod's orchard featuring blue ice on the frozen apple trees below a cloudy sky. Photographers submitted photos of familiar scenes made new with the coating of ice: a tire swing hanging from a sparkling tree, or a flock of lambs grazing in the middle of a frozen field. "I thought it was interesting," Kendra said of the photo of the lambs. "It was a frozen version of oil paintings you see quite often produced in this area."

At first, this beauty was mixed in with the horror of the storm and devastation in the streets, but after a while the reality of being without power overshadowed all else. A warm spell in the days following the storm melted the glistening ice off the trees and still the power was off. It was not the miracles of nature people wanted by then, but the conveniences of indoor electricity and heat.

By candle and lantern, Susan Newcomer completes a crossword puzzle without electricity in Spofford, New Hampshire.

ACT III
DEALING WITH DARKNESS, COPING WITH COLD

A Sullivan, New Hampshire, cabin on December 14.

Chapter 7
Yankee Ingenuity

"Were we prepared? No. But were we adaptable? Yes."
Adam Heintz, Wendell, Massachusetts

A central part of the Northeast mentality has always been perseverance and creativity in the face of adversity – Yankee ingenuity. When the ice storm swept through, schools closed, events were canceled, and businesses shut their doors. But people remained committed to what they felt was important, whether it was keeping their families warm, volunteering at shelters, or cutting and clearing brush out of neighbors' driveways. Across the Monadnock region and beyond, they found ways to press on under the weight of the ice. It was not a matter of if; it was a matter of how.

Scott Tolman's house is in a rural part of Chesterfield, New Hampshire, that lost power for just over a week. He and his family kept their horses alive by dragging water to their barn from a nearby pond, and kept warm themselves by constantly feeding their woodstove. It was under those conditions that the Tolman family prepared to celebrate their daughter Michaela's 18th birthday.

"There was never a moment I thought we'd cancel it," Scott said of his daughter's party. "It was a special day, and it needed to be a special day." The family mobilized to get together a surprise party for her birthday on December 13, two days after the storm. Using the family's woodstove and gas stove, Scott made exactly what Michaela had asked for her birthday dinner – beef stew with crunchy bread and lots of strawberries for dessert. Guests were invited, and although some could not make it, more than 20 showed up.

Aaron Howland, from Winchester, New Hampshire, was one of the guests. His town was relatively unscathed, and he was shocked to be driving over downed wires and tree branches on his way to the Tolman residence. When he arrived, the lights were off, and he hesitantly approached to knock on the door thinking they might not be home. He soon found out otherwise.

Inside, Aaron and the other guests ate and drank to candlelight. Staying close together and close to the fireplace for warmth, they talked and sang and had in all other respects a great party. In lieu of music from an electric sound system, Aaron sang for the rest of the guests. The party started just before 7 p.m. and the last guests stayed until 3 or 4 in the morning. "I was nervous that I had read the wrong information on the invitation," Aaron said. "I was surprised there was no power, and I was surprised that it went so well. But I shouldn't have put it past the Tolmans."

The Harrisville General Store has been in operation since 1838, but in the months before the ice storm, the owners were looking to get out of the business. The new owner, M'Lue Zahner, bought the business with her daughter and scheduled a grand reopening on December 12, alas for them, the day after the ice storm. The store was without power that morning, but M'Lue and her staff decided to have the opening as planned.

The store had no refrigeration, no running water, no lights, and no phone. Arriving at the store at 4 a.m., M'Lue carried a flashlight with her and lit candles. She cooked on a gas stove and a customer brought in water from a nearby natural spring for coffee. The store actually opened on time, at 7 a.m., and the customers started pouring in. M'Lue and her staff cooked them breakfast sandwiches and gave them a place to sit and have coffee. "Even though everything was hard to do, we were able to do it," M'Lue said. Residents came in throughout the day talking about their experiences in the storm until it started to seem like a party. By the end, M'Lue was ready to call it a successful first day.

Employee Shane Vanderbilt worked the counter, manned the gas stoves, and did whatever else was needed. In the midst of everything, he noticed people were having a good time. "As much as people were upset about the situation, they were really happy we were here and we were open," Shane remarked.

One event that found itself on the dark side of the ice storm had been in the making for 25 years. High school sweethearts Tim O'Connell and Kirsten Opdyke had dated while attending ConVal High School in Peterborough and then through college. They separated when Tim went on to architectural school while Kirsten wanted to start a family. Both had married someone else and both had eventually divorced. When they met up 15 years later, Kirsten was living in Dublin and Tim in Boston, but they knew it was meant to be. Tim proposed in November of 2008, and the wedding date was set for Saturday, December 20, at the Dublin Community Church.

When the ice storm hit on December 11, Kirsten thought the power would be back on by the following Monday. When Monday came and went without electricity, she began calling the church every day. By Wednesday, they started getting nervous, and on Thursday, they heard predictions for renewed inclement weather over the next two days. Kirsten's mother asked her what plan B was. Would they be married next to the woodstove at the house instead? After consulting with her fiancé, Kirsten informed her mother that there would be no plan B. "I've waited 25 years to marry you," Tim told Kirsten. "We're going to get married in that church!"

On their wedding day, the temperature in church was 17 degrees. Kirsten and Tim moved the ceremony to earlier in the afternoon, thinking it might be warmer, but still had to wait an hour for some relatives driving through the snowstorm outside. Finally, the 20 guests assembled inside and the ceremony began at 4 p.m. "We paused for a moment and looked back," Kirsten said. "All our family members were snuggled into the front pews. With the silence, and looking at their breath coming out, it gave you chills. There was no music, no traffic; there was a snowstorm, and no generators. Nobody had any power, but Tim and I didn't feel cold at all."

The pastor of the church, Mike Scott, drove up from Massachusetts through the blizzard to get there, and said this was the first wedding he performed where he could see his breath during the ceremony. He had prepared a long speech, but decided under the circumstances to cut it down to two sentences: "The indestructibility of this wedding ceremony in the face of almost unimaginable adversity suggests that the same might be true of the marriage. Make it so."

Power was restored to the church the next day.

Pastor Mike Scott, center, officiates at Kirsten and Tim O'Connell's wedding at the Dublin, New Hampshire, Community Church on December 20 without heat or electricity.

The *Ledger-Transcript* lost power along with everyone else in Peterborough, and without a generator, the editors and publisher had to figure out a way to get the paper to print. The *Ledger-Transcript* publishes on Tuesdays and Thursdays, and made a plan on Sunday for Monday's press deadline. Editors Marcia Patten and Steve Leone packed up the server computer and drove up to Concord with publisher Heather McKernan. Dave Anderson, the third editor, stayed behind to act as a liaison with reporters at Performance Health and Fitness, a Peterborough gym where power had already been restored.

Of all the reporters, only two of us had power. I was told to stay where I was and make calls from my apartment in Keene while other reporters were given laptops and worked out of the gym. Set up in a small office with spotty Internet access, Dave said he saw most of the reporters coming in and out all day. They came in, plugged into the wall, and sat next to the treadmills to type.

In Concord, Steve, Marcia, and Heather worked in a windowless room at the *Concord Monitor* facility to lay out the paper. They each had a computer, but they were not networked together. Only Steve worked on page layouts while the others edited stories, passing files back and forth using a thumb drive. Tundra Slosek, one of the company's computer technicians, was assigned to help them out, and set up an e-mail account where reporters could send stories and pictures. "We didn't have access to any of our computers or our newsroom or our e-mail," Steve said. "We didn't have any of our anything. It was kind of like survivalist journalism." Marcia, who got her start in the newspaper business in 1973, said that was one of the toughest production days of her career. In 1974, her newspaper's building burned to the ground, but getting that paper out had been easy compared to the ice storm, she said. At the end of the day, the *Ledger-Transcript* printed a 12-page paper with pictures and stories from the storm, about half the size of a normal Tuesday paper. Though all said it was difficult, none of the editors thought for a second the paper would fail to come out.

From all around the area of the ice storm came stories of parties, events, and businesses that were able to press on despite incredible odds. But outages wore on, and as days turned to weeks, even the hardiest New Englanders found that overcoming adversity would be a matter of sticking it out and reassessing what they took for granted.

A homemade heating system warms a living room in Merrimack, New Hampshire, on December 14.

Chapter 8
Taken for Granted: Heat

"The world narrowed down to wood and water."
Lisa Sieverts, Nelson, New Hampshire

Anyone who has lived through at least one true New England winter learns to be mindful of the two words "single digits" or the more intense "below zero." In most of the Monadnock region, residents spread these words around at least a few times each winter – frequent enough to be familiar and rare enough to be respected.

Temperatures danced up and down in the days following the ice storm as heat slowly leaked out of the homes that had lost power. A Peterborough woman, Marilyn Vose, tried to tough out the first few days in her apartment. The first morning was 50 degrees; the second was 40. "I didn't sleep much that night because it was so cold," Marilyn said. "I had to keep the blanket over my face to breathe." The next night, she bit the bullet and headed to her sister's house, which had a generator and a woodstove.

For many, woodstoves meant the difference between sticking it out at home or searching for shelter. Oil furnaces stopped working without power, and the wood pellet stoves that were supposed to save owners hundreds of dollars on oil were likewise dependent on electricity. Homeowners whose woodstoves had been unused for decades found themselves thankful they had kept them around.

While others were shivering under blankets and rubbing their hands together to keep them warm, Mitch Call had to open the door to his A-frame house in Sharon, New Hampshire, because his woodstove sent the inside temperature up to 85 degrees. Mitch's problem came three days after the storm when he ran out of wood, and he invited himself up to his ex-wife's house to await the return of power.

A lack of wood was one problem Peterborough selectwoman Elizabeth Thomas did not have. She lives in a remote farmhouse that has been in her family since the 1930s. "We have the woodstove and there's wood in the basement," she said. "This is a working farm. We were self-sufficient then and there's no reason we can't be now." Elizabeth's house has a furnace, but she often uses her woodstove to heat her kitchen and dining room. The woodstove had been a heat source in that house since she was a child.

Along with the other selectmen, Elizabeth spent many nights volunteering at the Peterborough shelter at the South Meadow School. Locals without heat flocked there, she said, seeking a place to be warm.

For those without power, gathering wood and feeding the stove became a ritual that had to be performed every three or four hours. Keeping warm was a constant effort, filling the days and nights with the chore of stoking. Interrupted nights of sleep were a common story.

Pam Crook of Greenfield, New Hampshire, found herself stacking wood, an activity she rarely, if ever, performed. Her husband was up every two hours to feed their two woodstoves. When they bought their house 13 years before, a pile of wood came with it, and most of it stayed right where it was all that time. After several days without power, Pam's husband had to go out and get more. "Just finding firewood was a big deal," Pam said. She and her family kept warm enough, but sadly her tropical fish, Oscar, went belly up.

Some people heated with wood, and some with propane, but others had nothing at all and stayed home anyway. Melissa Lee and her parents in Westmoreland, New Hampshire, lived in a new house without a woodstove. She worked at her parents' laundromat in Keene during the day, but at night, she returned home to a cold house. "We all slept in the same room and had tons of blankets," Melissa said.

Laura Fletcher never had a thought of leaving her home. She had a woodstove and plenty of wood to go with it, but she used it in a

Laura Fletcher clears her car in Stoddard, New Hampshire. Losing power was nothing new for her, as she lived without electricity for seven years.

way that would ensure it would last. At 76 years old, Laura lives well off the beaten path in Stoddard. I found her only when I got lost looking for someone else, and she agreed to speak with me as she shoveled her walk and brushed the newly fallen snow off her car.

She said that one morning while she didn't have power, the inside of her house got as low as 18 degrees. She dealt with it because she knows how to dress, she said, and she has good cold-weather clothes. "I like the solitude and like being by myself," she said. "I resent when I have to leave the house, so being here was no problem."

When she found the place in the 1970s, she fell in love with it, even though there was no electricity in the house. For her first seven and a half years there, she lived without power. In those early days, she said she had to hike to the house and back from where the road used to end, carrying supplies in a back pack. During the ice storm, she said, she was never afraid, even as trees blocked the way out and she lost her phone. "I'm prepared for emergencies out here," she said, brushing the last of the snow from her car as the sun set behind us.

A teardrop-shaped ice formation on a branch in Readsboro, Vermont, on December 13.

Chapter 9
Taken for Granted: Water

"I had to truck in water. It was not like
you could just walk 15 feet and there it was."
Stephanie Fitzpatrick, Red Hook, New York

Heating the body was imperative for survival, but the first thought that came to most homeowners was heating their pipes. The dropping temperatures at night created the potential for bursting pipes, and the ensuing water damage.

Lisa Sieverts of Nelson, New Hampshire, awoke at 1 a.m. the night of the storm and said, "Oh, no" without knowing why. It was a few moments later she realized the power was out and decided to start the woodstoves. She and Max Nunnemaker were warm in bed, but in her basement, the temperature was already beginning to drop. The problem for Lisa and Max was that the stove was above the pipes they were trying to keep warm. "We were keeping the woodstoves at full blast for 10 days, trying to heat the basement from the first floor, going against the laws of physics," Lisa said. She went through her allotted wood for the entire winter in just two weeks, keeping the house warmer than it usually would have been, but the basement temperature still dropped to 32 degrees after nine days. Defeated, she drained the pipes.

As the water cooled in the pipes, Lisa and Max filled up gal-

Ice-covered pine trees in Sullivan, New Hampshire, on the day after the storm.

lon jugs at a nearby creek for dish and toilet water, which proved dangerous early on. During one trip to the creek, Lisa brought four jugs down, but could only carry two back at a time. As she got to the edge of the woods carrying her first load, she heard a loud crack above her. Dropping the water, Lisa raced forward and dove onto the lawn. A branch crashed to the ground less than 10 feet behind her. Shaken, Lisa picked up the two jugs she had dropped and left the other two down by the creek.

Many people near town centers subsisted on gravity-fed town

STILL PREPARED: A month after the storm, several jugs of drinking water sit next to a stack of fire wood piled in front of the woodstove at Lisa Sieverts' house in Nelson, New Hampshire.

water, but those with wells had to make other arrangements. Henry Bley-Vroman, living with his grandmother in Alstead, New Hampshire, went down to their dug well and pulled up water with buckets three times each day. The house at one time had been a vacation home without electricity, and had a hand pump in the kitchen, but that had been taken out when the house was wired.

Water was a touchy subject in Alstead, which three years earlier had experienced catastrophic flooding resulting in heavy property damage and several deaths. The Cold River, which overflowed its banks in 2005, had since been fitted with an artificial, cinderblock-lined channel to prevent flooding. The heavy rains from the ice storm brought the water level to the channel's brim. "It was definitely interesting seeing it get its first test," Henry said.

At both Henry and Lisa's houses, water was heated for doing dishes, a task they said took three times as long as normal. Some households, like Melissa Lee's, had strict water regimens. Melissa's parents grew up in Korea and knew how to get the most out of every drop. "It was first for the vegetables, second for dishes, and then it went to the toilet," Melissa said.

Rivers and streams, like this one in Otis, Massachusetts, became water sources for some without power.

Had the ice storm happened a year earlier, Ron and Tiger Waterman from Readsboro, Vermont, would have had it easy. With a woodstove and gravity-fed water, they were already in good shape, but before the winter came, they had switched from a gas-powered water heating system to an electric one. So, like so many others, they had to look elsewhere for showers.

Some showered in shelters, some at gyms where lines would form, and some at friends' houses who still had power or who had generators. Most often, showers were not an everyday occurrence. "It was a once every two or three days thing," said Elice Laughner of Nelson, who hauled cold water from a stream near her cabin each day, sometimes having to shovel through several inches of snow to get at it.

After six days without power, Lisa and Max learned from a neighbor to use baby wipes as a way to wash their hands without using water. Not having showered in a long time, when Lisa went out in public, she used a "funny hat" as an improvised disguise.

Deb Giaimo of Dublin, New Hampshire, took sponge baths with water she heated on her woodstove rather than stand in line at the gym. "I was feeling grubby and had limited time and I couldn't do it," Deb said. "You almost become desperate. You're so tired at that point, physically and mentally tired of constantly trying to keep your head above water."

Deb's words had an even greater meaning for those with sump pumps in their basements. Sump pump owners depend on electricity to keep their basements from becoming flooded, and without it, they had to bail themselves out the old-fashioned way. In Spofford, the situation in Sue Marland's basement was so bad it took her two hours to empty it with buckets, and it had to be done every few hours. Climbing up and down the stairs over and over, Sue used the water flooding the basement to flush her toilets. Balanced against that responsibility was the need to spend time with her daughter, who has special needs. "She is so connected to anything electric," Sue said. "It was driving her crazy. The only thing that worked for her was a portable DVD player. She was the happiest she was all week long with that until the batteries ran out."

Sue was driven crazy by her own lack of water, and eventually went to friends' houses to use the shower and warm up. She couldn't leave her house for long because of her animals. After two and a half days of bailing out the water, she was able to borrow a generator, which she immediately hooked up to the sump pump.

The relative scarcity of water bore down on people as the outages continued. As power flickered and came on for hours at a time, Deb, Melissa, and others did what they did not have a chance to do the first time around – they filled their bathtubs with water, ready to hold out for longer if necessary.

A frozen apple hangs from the tree at Carter Hill Orchard in Concord, New Hampshire, on December 14.

Chapter 10
Taken for Granted: Food

"Let's just say it was all of it."
**Bill Burt, manager of Little Roy's Convenience Store,
Peterborough, NH, on how much perishable food was lost**

At the same time those without power fought to keep their pipes and their bodies warm, they also fought to keep their food cold. In the Monadnock region, this was especially true for Dave Westover, a commercial ice cream maker in Walpole, New Hampshire. Normally, his stock is refrigerated at 20 below.

Thinking quickly after they lost power, Dave and his staff loaded everything they had into the back of their freezer delivery truck. It took them more than three hours to move it all; Dave estimates there were between 3,000 and 4,000 pints.

His power was restored relatively quickly, and Dave and his crew found themselves moving the ice cream back into the freezer after only a matter of hours. "I wouldn't want to move it every day, and that day we had to do it twice, but we were fortunate we had that option," Dave said. "If we hadn't had the ability to move it into the delivery truck we would have lost everything, or we would have had one heck of an ice cream block party that night."

In Jaffrey, Liz Hardison got her family together to take them to her parents' house in Gardner, Massachusetts. When she got to Dunkin' Donuts, where she thought she would be able to get coffee, she found the city without power. She booked a room at the Super 8 Motel in Keene, securing one of the last three rooms available.

Across the street from the motel was the Olive Garden that Liz managed. The motel and restaurant, like most of Keene, had power. Though she had the weekend off, she called the restaurant right away to have her cooks prepare as much food as possible. On one day, she asked for 15 pans of pasta with sauce that fed 10 people each, along with 15 jumbo salads and more than 200 breadsticks. Another day it was pans of chicken marsala, mashed potatoes, and 20 gallons of various kinds of soups. She had lasagnas prepared as well. All of the food was donated to the shelter in Rindge. "I had the ability to help people," Liz said. "I had a whole restaurant with tons of food at my disposal. I just wanted to help."

At shelters across the Monadnock region and beyond, many more people stopped in for meals and temporary warmth than stayed overnight. Liz picked the Rindge shelter because it was the only shelter she knew about at the time. The shelter in Jaffrey, her own town, had not registered with state police. Liz made food runs down to Rindge on Saturday, Sunday, Monday, and Wednesday. Her restaurant was the only Olive Garden under her regional director of operations that had power. The other five, all in Massachusetts, could not open.

Inside, business was booming, and Liz waited for downtimes before asking her staff to prepare food for the shelter, which took two hours. Talking to customers, Liz found that many were from surrounding towns without power, eating out because there was no food at home or no way to cook it. Between 9 p.m. and 9:30 p.m. was another boom in business, when Public Service of New Hampshire line workers would come in groups of 50 to 100, eating on the company credit card.

Almost everyone without a generator who lost power for some duration emptied their refrigerators and freezers. Those who could applied an adage long celebrated in the Yankee mindset: "waste not, want not." But many were forced to discard most, if not all, of their perishable food. For those who had them, cooking could be accomplished on woodstoves or gas stoves. Others ate their meals cold.

Debbie Lindsey of Hubbardston, Massachusetts, drove up to Rindge on Sunday to grocery shop, but none of the supermarkets had any ice. When she came home with lots of canned goods, she placed some of the perishables already in her fridge in a cooler outside the house. Because there was no ice to be bought, she chipped some off of the farm equipment behind her house and threw it in with the food she wanted to keep cold. "We tried to eat all we could of the freezer stuff, and discarded the rest," she said, adding that she thought Americans, who buy non-perishables, are better suited to this kind of emergency than Europeans, who often shop day-to-day.

Marcia Patten, senior editor at the *Ledger-Transcript*, was not so prepared. She and her husband, Roland, had planned to go out for breakfast in Peterborough the morning after the storm, and found to their surprise that there was no food to be had in town and the roads were too treacherous to venture very far. "We came back here and we had a jar of peanut butter, and that's what we ate along with water for our breakfast," Marcia said.

For another *Ledger-Transcript* editor, Dave Anderson, the problem was too much food. He and his wife Kathy emptied their freezer and kept their food outside for a few days until the temperature warmed up. Their power came back just in time to save most of it. They cooked pizzas and soups on their woodstove, and Kathy used up blueberries that had been stored from the summer.

By December 22, berries frozen for the winter at Lisa Seiverts' home in Nelson, New Hampshire, had thawed out and had to be used right away.

Public Service of New Hampshire employees eat dinner at Energy Park in Manchester, New Hampshire, on December 16.

Down the road from the Andersons in downtown Hancock, a community supper that had been planned in advance for the night of December 12 went on as planned. Ham had been cooked ahead of time and organizers scrambled to find people with woodstoves or other ways to cook the food that had been set aside. "That all went down to the church vestry in town," Dave said. "Quite a few people showed up, and it was a good meal."

As power was being restored to the large chain supermarkets on the state highways, and as those brave enough to try the roads flocked to Keene or other places where there was still electricity, town general stores did the best they could to open, too. Roy's Market in Peterborough was open for at least a part of every day, even when they did not have power. Bill Burt, the store manager of the sister store down the street, Little Roy's, worked at the store escorting customers around with a flashlight. Prices were written down and added up with a grease pencil because there were no computers.

There was markedly less business, but there were still lines out the door because the store could accommodate only a few people at a time in the darkness. "The customers were wonderful," Bill said. "They were appreciative we were open and making the best of

Public Service of New Hampshire hired area restaurants and caterers to serve meals to workers.

what we had to sell. They bought baked beans, tuna fish, and maybe even a can of spam, things you could make a meal out of without electricity at your home." The staff at Roy's took no chances with any of the meat or dairy products, tossing them all. It was several days before they were able to restock, and restoring the contents of the empty freezers took multiple deliveries.

Home from the store with food on the table, most dined by candlelight.

Tiger Waterman wears her headlamp outside of her Readsboro, Ver-mont, home the day after the storm.

Chapter 11
Taken for Granted: Light

*"I think the most interesting thing was how
dark it got with no ambient light anywhere."*

**Richard Dunning, principal, South Meadow School,
Peterborough, New Hampshire**

The village of Red Hook, New York, serves as a small center of commerce in northern Dutchess County on the east side of the Hudson River Valley. The center of town is not a church or a town hall; it is a traffic light at the busy intersection of state highways 9 and 199. Further lighting the lamppost-lined roads, it is as much a defining landmark as the historic diner a few blocks up Route 9 or the nearby multiplex movie theater. On the evening of December 11, as Red Hook humane law officer Stephanie Fitzpatrick waited for the light to change from red to green, everything went black.

The center of town was dark for a few days, and Stephanie's house was out for much longer. Police officers directed traffic in the darkness, visible only because of headlights, until power was restored. Red Hook found itself among the worst affected areas in New York State.

Peterborough, likewise a commercial center, was also a place of darkness in the days following the storm, meaning that people looking for sustenance after the sun had set found a ghost town. "It's amazing how dark the downtown was," said Peterborough Public Works Director Rodney Bartlett. "I'm not sure eerie is the correct word, but it was such a dramatic change from even a quiet night. When the sun went down, there was no real activity."

Early into the outages, among the only lights that could be seen was the "Open" sign on the Peterborough Diner. Restaurant manager Mike Stone lived in neighboring Greenfield, but while the power was out, he stayed at the diner 24 hours a day. Using a generator, he opened at 1 p.m. on the Saturday after the storm. "My sign on my roof was lit; I made sure it was lit," Mike said. "I wanted people driving around to see we were open so they could come and eat." As Mike ran the diner, customers would come in telling him they had seen a glow in the sky and followed it to see what it was. They gratefully ordered hot meals and hot drinks. Mike had never seen anything like it. In his 12 years with the diner, a period of time that included the large 1998 ice storm and an enormous flood in 2007, he had never seen power out in downtown Peterborough for more than a few hours.

While those who lost power often talked about the stress of the approach of December 25, the winter solstice date of December 22 presented a further hardship – the outages occurred during the darkest time of the year. Deb Giaimo of Dublin, New Hampshire, said she did all she could to use the daylight hours, particularly household chores. "You'd be sweeping the rugs in the dark, and sweeping rugs in the dark is not efficient," Deb said with a laugh.

In the evenings, many people used light-emitting diode (LED) headlamps to read or to get around the house. Flashlights were also used by people who had them and the batteries to make them work, but flashlights, batteries, and candles were some of the hottest items in stores, and shortly after the ice storm subsided, they were all but impossible to find.

Lisa Sieverts tried to head into Keene to find plumber's candles several days into the outage at her house in Nelson. Plumber's candles, in Lisa's mind, were the perfect provision – inexpensive, long lasting, and clean burning without much dribbling wax. Not only were stores out of plumber's candles, the only candles they had left were for lavender-scented aromatherapy. Desperate, Lisa grabbed a five-dollar candle from Pier One. "I just wanted a white candle," she said. "It was ridiculous."

At Edmunds' Hardware Store in Antrim, Rick Edmunds sold out a case of 288 plumber's candles in two days. He sold out of D batteries and lamp oil the first day after the storm, along with generator supplies. The store itself did not have lights, so Rick and his staff used flashlights to bring customers around. Rick's own house in Antrim lost power as well, and his young sons, ages 2 and 4, had a blast playing with flashlights. "They did fine," Rick said of his kids. "Little boys like flashlights."

While the Edmunds boys were playing with their flashlights, Louise Rath of Spofford was trying to figure out how to work hers. Buying several at a local store right after the storm, she brought them home and, unfamiliar with them, did not know that a plastic cover had to be removed. "None of us could figure out how to put the battery in the flashlight and make it work," she said.

Many commented on how the darkness affected their sleep cycles. People who normally ate dinner at 6 p.m. found themselves hungry at 4:30, and people who went to bed at 10 or 11 at night started turning in at 8, or even earlier.

Henry Bley-Vroman from Alstead usually stayed up until 1 or 2 in the morning before the ice storm hit, a habit that did not continue during the outage. "I wouldn't have been surprised if I had been tired at 10, but to be thinking about bed at 8, and to be ready for dinner by 5 o'clock was surprising and fascinating," Henry said. "It felt like I was being released into the sleep/wake pattern that was more the natural default."

By the dim light of candles, visibility was shortened. During those long nights, lights that would illuminate entire rooms hung uselessly from ceilings while small glowing flames wobbled on windowsills and tables beneath them. Moving from room to room, the powerless flicked switches out of habit and felt silly when they realized nothing would happen. Returning to flickering candles, they found themselves sitting closer to light sources and closer together.

Louise Rath, center, and her husband, Dan, right, hold a get together at their house in Spofford, New Hampshire, on January 18, 2009, for all of their neighbors who visited during the storm.

Chapter 12
Communication and Community

*"It brings people together in ways you wouldn't expect.
People are segregated with iPods and cell phones.
It's good to see people coming together, drinking coffee,
and talking to each other for the first time in a long time."*

Steve Lindsey, state representative, Keene, New Hampshire

While the storm made people focus on their personal needs, like heat and water, one of its most drastic impacts was on communication. Phone lines were brought down. Access to the Internet was mostly non-existent. Cell phone towers failed. Blocked roads and smashed cars made traveling to population centers difficult, and in many cases, store closures made the trips fruitless anyway.

As long-distance communication broke down, however, communities blossomed. Neighbors who had never spoken to one another were suddenly dependent on each other. Local police and fire departments spread news to residents by going door to door. Those who had power, or generators, or water, or anything useful to others, found themselves going to great lengths to assist neighbors. For many, the only way to "reach out and touch someone" was to offer or to take a helping hand.

An ice covered antenna sags on top of a house in Sullivan, New Hampshire, on the day after the storm.

Cynthia Geary, a Francestown, New Hampshire, resident during the storm, had spent most of her life before then down south in Virginia. Taking a job with Peterborough-based Monadnock Music brought her into a rural environment in which she lived alone. While she had contacts in the music world across the globe, she had precious few neighbors nearby.

The night of the storm, she heard branches falling, and was not the only person to observe that they pounded the ground "like Godzilla." When she peeked her head out the next morning, everything smelled like pine. Wood was splintered everywhere and the two utility poles on her property were leaning over from safety cables snapping and huge branches having landed on the wires. She had lost power at 1:49 a.m. according to her cell phone clock, and it would be nearly a week before she got it back.

Trying to stick it out through what she thought would be a matter of hours without power, Cynthia let a prepared pile of wood sit unburned in her fireplace all through the first day, but when night fell and there was still no sign of power, she gave in and lit the match. From that moment until her power was restored, she stoked the fire every hour on the hour unless she was outside hauling wood. Though this was a lonely labor, Cynthia found her way over to her neighbor's house for company during the hard times.

"If it were not for my neighbor Sara Cox and her family, who were very kind to me, I might have gone mad," Cynthia said. "Two days after the storm, on that 54 degree balmy day, I decided I was going to walk down the road to see what everyone else was doing. It was a forced vacation because I could do no work. The loss of productivity was excruciating for me because I love my work. I walked down the road and I knocked on her door. We had met in town a couple of times. We just sat down and had coffee; she reassured me that everything would be okay. Even though I lived alone, I wasn't alone."

Every few days, Cynthia visited the Cox family, who helped her out by buying groceries and gas. The night before the power returned to their street, Sara invited Cynthia to join her daughter, Greta, who was volunteering for a spaghetti supper in Peterborough. Cynthia agreed. Fire department crews from all over the region came to the supper, but were called out in the middle. The chef kept the supper warm until they could return. "It was very invigorating," she said. "And I realized that even when things feel really rough, it is true that if you transport yourself into the mode of thinking of other people and helping other people, you feel a great sense of community and forget all of your troubles." A month after the storm, Cynthia still kept up with the Cox family, attending Sara's birthday party in late January. A Grammy Award winning musician, Cynthia wrote a song for the party in honor of Sara.

Community suppers became popular social outlets in the days and weeks after the storm. In Hancock, as previously mentioned, a supper planned for the night of December 12 went on as planned, allowing residents to get together and eat with one another. Andrew and Michelle Freeman, owners of the Dublin Village Store, hosted a free turkey supper at the local elementary school when they got their power back. With lines out the door, they served 225 meals. The community was so grateful that three months later Andrew and Michelle were named the town's Citizens of the Year.

In the Monadnock region, some towns completely lost phone service, and in many cases, phones were out longer than electricity. Phone service providers had to wait while first tree crews, then electricity workers, repaired lines before fixing their own service.

Sue Shorrock of New Ipswich was without phone service for four weeks and got a cell phone for the first time. Far from enamored with the new piece of technology, she was completely disgusted. I spoke with her the day she got her land-line service back and she was as pleased as could be to have a "real" phone again. "It's nice not to have to talk on something the size of a Reese's Peanut Butter Cup," she said. Continuing the candy bar metaphor, she added, "I'm happy not to shell out any more money on this almond bar."

Jim Van Dongen, public information officer for the New Hampshire Division of Homeland Security and Emergency, named communications as one of the greatest challenges of the recovery effort. The state's major TV station, WMUR-TV (Channel 9), was off the air for several hours. Even when it came back on the air, most viewers were unable to receive the station, either because they or their cable providers were still without power. Emergency management officials used the state's Emergency Alert System, which sends emergency messages through all of the state's radio and TV media. Messages had to be kept to less than 90 seconds, which was barely long enough to remind people to seek shelter if they were without power or warn them of the dangers of carbon monoxide poisoning.

Peterborough Public Works Director Rodney Bartlett quickly became frustrated with Public Service of New Hampshire's restoration effort due to a lack of communication. He could not get through to the New Hampshire Department of Homeland Security until Monday evening, three days into the crisis. "Our lack of ability to communicate created a sense that things were okay in the Monadnock region," Rodney said. But things were not okay. As utility crews got the northern and seacoast areas quickly back online, Monadnock Community Hospital remained on generator power for four days. Peterborough Town Administrator Pam Brenner got on the phone with the governor's office to express concerns about the situation in Peterborough. When Governor John Lynch learned this, he called back within 15 minutes.

The governor responded with a visit to Peterborough on Tuesday, along with U.S. Representative Paul Hodes and the vice president of PSNH. They viewed the shelter at the South Meadow School and met with town officials, who tried to describe Peterborough's commercial importance to the region. "Because those services weren't there, there was no ability to even help the residents of Peterborough or the surrounding communities," Rodney said. "To get gas for a generator, you had to drive 25 or 30 miles. PSNH did not appreciate what a level of disaster and devastation we were in." The trip sparked a response. By Wednesday, PSNH committed to sending "an armada" of service trucks to the region.

Linda Lawrence's car was crushed during the storm in Wells, Maine. The crash was so loud, she thought that her house had been hit.

In the meantime, folks were cut off from the outside world. Residents in some towns reported robberies at this vulnerable time, and town officials called in the National Guard. In other places, residents who had few ways to travel or communicate banded together creating miniature communities.

One such community developed in Spofford. Louise Rath and her husband Dan had heat and a generator which provided hot, running water. With these conveniences, Dan and Louise scoured the neighborhood to offer help. They gathered a group, many of whom they had rarely spoken with. Many had problems with flooded basements and no sump pumps. They put up their neighbor, Bobbie Petrovitch, in a spare room and drove around knocking on people's doors to see who else needed help.

Most said they didn't need help, falling back on the old Yankee independent spirit, but duration cracked a few. A week into the outages, more than 10 neighbors were using the Raths' shower and stopping by on a regular basis to warm up. A month after the outages ended, they all got together again to reminisce about the storm. "I finally gave in," Sue Marland recalled at the gathering. "I was trying to hold out, but not having water really drives me crazy."

Sarah Cooper-Ellis was relatively new to the neighborhood, having only lived there two years. Louise's offers of help connected her in a substantial way with those around her. "I really wanted to feel connected and know who my neighbors were," Sarah said. "I wanted to feel like I live here in a deeper way. For me it was an excuse, an opportunity to make relationships with people. Plus, I think because I live by myself, I don't feel like I can know all the things I need to do. I didn't know whether I should leave the breaker on or off. The ice storm allowed me to accept help, and I have a hard time doing that often. I thought, 'I'm just going to say yes.' 'Do you want to come over for Chinese take-out?' 'Yes.' 'Do you want me to do your laundry?' 'Yes.'"

One of the Raths' tenants was Jose Macias, a student and baseball player at nearby Franklin Pierce University in Rindge. Hailing from the Bronx, Jose had never experienced an ice storm before, much less one causing such devastation with trees strewn across the roads. Finals were canceled and students were encouraged to get off campus any way they could. Jose's father was unable to get him, so Dan, a friend of the family, picked him up instead and brought him over to Spofford. "In one building there were 100 people in a small-sized room," Jose said of the arrangements on campus. "I didn't want to stay there." Jose and Dan started a nightly ritual of playing pool in the dim candlelight of the game room as the sun went down.

Franklin Pierce and a few other colleges were evacuated, but some other communities stayed together. Tali Fridman at Camphill Village in Copake, New York described how her household, made up of developmentally disabled adults and their caretakers, stuck together. "The power went out and we thought, 'Uh oh, hope it comes back soon,'" Tali said. Copake is located in Columbia County, which New York emergency management officials deemed the hardest hit county in the state. Tali's own house narrowly missed being struck by a large willow tree nearby.

Living with residents very sensitive to changes in routine made the outage difficult. Some residents complained about the lack of heat. People had to go without showers, and laundry piled up. In order to help residents brush their teeth and perform other tasks, Tali and others used headlamps, and many houses in the village purchased generators. The dangers of falling limbs meant keeping people inside for the early part of the outage. Some sat quietly, some had difficulty being unoccupied, and some were scared.

Thane Page stands by his FairPoint Communications truck a month after the storm. He worked 12-hour shifts repairing phone lines from December 11 through the end of 2008.

While she was happy the outage didn't last longer than a few days, Tali recognized there were some good aspects to the storm for her community. "In a way it was more hectic because we had to keep people warm and manage without electricity, but it was quieter as a result," she said. "We just gathered in the living room and it brought us together in a really sweet way. I think we managed quite well. Thinking about it, things could have been much worse."

Another community strongly affected was Peterborough's Mac-Dowell Colony, the oldest artist colony in America. Featuring secluded studios in the woods for each artist with a residency, the colony was extremely vulnerable to the falling limbs and downed wires. At more than 100 years old, the colony also has the distinction of surviving the hurricane of 1938. World famous American composer Aaron Copeland was staying at the colony at that time and described the aftermath as a "desolate, war-torn swamp." According to the MacDowell Colony's centennial memoir at the Library of Congress, it took two men with axes more than two hours to cut through downed trees and rescue the score he was working on for the ballet "Billy the Kid."

The 2008 ice storm affected MacDowell in a similar way but with greater impact on the residents as 70 years has much increased our culture's dependence on electricity. Colony spokesman Brendan Tapley said, "The two main promises we make to artists are that they won't be disturbed and they will have a private studio. Those two things were compromised. While they still had uninterrupted time here, the crisis was so much in the foreground that you couldn't relax and work on something. Survival needs trumped creative needs. That was the real price for the MacDowell."

Usually housing 32 artists, MacDowell's numbers dwindled to seven as artists left to find places with power and heat. Among the seven was one artist who could not leave if she wanted to. Alexandra Gardner, a musician from the Washington D.C. area, became stranded when a tree limb smashed through her car's roof, totaling it.

Normally artists at the colony are used to working individually during the day, but the dim light prevented productivity. In Alexandra's case, so did preoccupation with her car. The artists who stayed found themselves spending more time with one another and with the staff, who usually have only limited contact with the artists. "We invited the kitchen staff to have dinner with us and have fun," Alexandra said. "That was a very nice result of the event." A graphic artist who was among the seven who stayed made a T-shirt that read "We survived the ice storm." The other artists signed it. Like the hurricane of 1938, the ice storm is likely something the colony will remember for a long time. As for Alexandra, she said the next time she applies for a residency at MacDowell, she will ask for a summer stay.

Stores and restaurants on generators and those that got power back early became communities of their own, like Donna Robertson's coffee shop in Windham, New Hampshire. She lost power from Thursday night until Monday. With a refrigerator filled with milk products and four freezers with ice and food to take care of, Donna said it was complete chaos from the moment the outage started. She emptied the freezers right away. On Saturday night, when the temperature was in the single digits, she put the food on the front porch. During warmer days, she stuffed as much as she could into friends' freezers.

When the power came back on at 12:30 in the afternoon on Monday, she sprang into action. "I wanted to get the shop to be open for people who still didn't have any power, and within half an hour, I had the shop open," Donna said. "I brought in the employees that could help me the best. We were repacking the freezer and making people drinks."

With the holiday season accounting for 40 percent of her business, Donna knew she had to do whatever she could to stay open. Those without power came in for drinks, warmth, and links to civilization. Donna said even a week later she was hearing stories of people still without electricity. "You could hear in their voices how they were struggling and how much we rely on the power," she said. "When you get to the point where you don't have it and how people survive, to hear about it was heart-wrenching at times. A really good friend of mine had a chimney fire and had a lot of damage. They were trying to use the chimney for heat and they were without their home for a week after that to clean the soot out of their house." As Donna observed, everyone had something happen to them. Three willow trees on her property she had watched grow since her childhood were all destroyed. As her regulars returned, she posted updates she found online as to when power would be restored, trying to keep customers' hopes up.

At the Sharon Arts Center Exhibition Gallery in downtown Peterborough, gallery manager Kendra McGhee managed sales while people in outlying towns were still without power. One conversation she had really stuck with her. "One gentleman came in and he was older, probably in his retirement years and he was buying a Christmas gift for his wife," Kendra said. "I saw a picture of his dog when he pulled out his credit card and said, 'Oh, that looks like my dog I had when I was growing up.' He said he had to put her down a few weeks ago. It was a very sad story, and it started this conversation about what we have and what we take for granted. You don't realize how significant things are until you lose them. He still didn't have power back yet and said it was nice to shop in a nice, warm place. It was really encouraging." Kendra said that others came and went who were angry at the world, as it was impossible to be mad at any one person, but people like this man were just grateful to come in and have a conversation.

While human contact got people through some rough spots, it was electricity they wanted most of all. While many came up with creative ways around it, those who could found generators, which following the ice storm was an act that likewise required creativity.

At Edmunds' Hardware Store in Antrim, New Hampshire, store manager Rick Edmunds stands by the generator he has kept in stock since the rush following the ice storm.

Chapter 13
Generating Generators

"When you live on a lake, everything echoes, and I could hear the hums of the generators all around."
Chris Young, Stoddard, New Hampshire

With the grid down and power out, people looked for alternative sources of electricity, namely, generators. For those without wood stoves, the worry was that pipes would freeze; for those without water pumps, the need for water took precedence; and for everyone, there were the innumerable little missing conveniences we rely on every day whose source is electricity.

People who owned generators and maintained them regularly had a short trip to the shed to fire them up. But not everyone was so lucky. Don Primrose of Sullivan, New Hampshire, found his 10-year-old generator had a rusted-out fuel tank. When he called to see when he could get the part replaced, the hardware store told him he'd have to wait until the 16th of January.

Luckily for Glenn Joziatis and his wife Melanie in Merrimack, New Hampshire, their generator was working. Melanie is dependent on an electric oxygen machine to breathe, and Glenn plugs in a breathing machine at night when he sleeps. During the outage, their generator ran all day and all night for six days.

Glenn is the type that always has a backup plan. His wife's ma-

Taken in October, two months before the storm, this photo shows Ogion Fulford's solar-powered yurt in Guilford, Vermont, a town that saw heavy storm damage.

chine has a number of different power sources, and there is an oxygen storage tank as well with six to eight hours of air inside. The main machine condenses oxygen from ambient air. "I joke that it gives her oxygen while taking it away from me," Glenn said. A few days after the storm, Glenn returned home to find the generator had shut itself off and his wife's machine was running on back-up battery power. Thinking quickly, he found a minor breaker failure in the generator and was able to fix it.

Many, however, did not have a generator that December 11. When people saw how bad the devastation was and realized the power might be out for some time, it set off a mass scramble for generators. Hardware stores quickly found themselves out of stock.

One of the places people went in great numbers was The Home Depot in Keene. Norm Sturgeon, the assistant manager, said that

After the storm, Ogion Fulford's solar panels functioned, even with icicles hanging off of them, allowing him to live with the same amount of electricity he had before the storm."

generators sold out immediately, but that trucks replacing stock were sent right away. Friday, the day after the storm, was Norm's day off, and when he returned on Saturday, there were 200 people in the store waiting for generators. The only information available even to Norm was that a truck would be coming in the middle of the afternoon with a shipment of generators. Norm created a numbering system with his business cards from 1 to 200 guaranteeing those who got there first a generator when the truck arrived. Some waited all day long, through mid-afternoon until closing time. And the truck still had not come. "They were standing in a big group just waiting," Norm said of the customers. "None of them had power, so they had nowhere else to be anyway." Not if they wanted to stay warm.

Most of the customers were surprisingly understanding, and they left with the promise that they would be given priority when the truck arrived. A few were visibly upset. Norm and his staff told them they would get a phone call the next day if the truck arrived, and that their numbers would still be good.

The long-awaited truck arrived that night after closing, and customers started coming in as soon as the store opened the next day. Employees broke down pallets of generators as fast as they could, trying to appease the mad rush of customers. Norm said he had never seen anything like the business after the ice storm, and was amazed at and proud of the teamwork within the store. "The compassion people had for the customers went beyond just doing business," Norm said. "People wanted to be heroes for those customers." Staff members from every department asked to be in front, breaking down generator crates for people and carrying them to their cars. They had to explain how to hook them up so many times that every employee became an expert. When things had settled down again, The Home Depot in Keene found that it had sold 700 generators.

One Spofford resident had to resort to secrecy to get the last generator at a store in Winchester through her friend's husband, who was one of the store's regulars. When she showed up with her friends, the place was teeming with customers, but they were able to keep the deal quiet. "It was all hush-hush, who was going to get the last generator," she said. "They were all pretending and talking in code." The price was $677, and she let out a "holy sh-t" before taking out her credit card to pay for it. Two workers from the store came out to her car to load it up and show her how it worked. When everything was properly stowed, she hit the gas and got out of there.

Many borrowed generators from friends who had power, and some passed generators around, sharing the power among two or three homes. Tim Grossi, facilities director for the ConVal School District for Peterborough and the surrounding towns, did what many in his position had to do: load generators on the back of pickups and drive them around from building to building. Of the 11 school buildings in the district, nine were without power. "We knew we were in for a long haul," Tim said. "The fear became that without power, we had no heat and we have all of these sprinkler pipes. If it dips below 32 degrees, you're running the risk of those freezing up" and then exploding as the water expands into ice.

Tim broke his crew into teams to cover the nine buildings, having them spend an hour or two heating up each one. Some, like Francestown and Greenfield Elementary Schools, were nearly impossible to access due to road conditions, but Tim said his crew was up for the challenge. They worked from 5 or 6 in the morning until 8 or 9 at night, he said.

Having the generator was one thing, but getting the fuel for it

A generator sits outside a Peterborough, New Hampshire, garage on December 20.

was another. Chris Pfeil from Lyndeborough, New Hampshire, waited in line for 30 minutes at a gas station in Hillsborough, New Hampshire, the first day after the storm. No one was filling up their cars, he said. It was all people with gas cans.

Carr's Store, a gas station in Dublin, New Hampshire, learned its lesson from losing power in the ice storm in 1998 and had a generator. That was the only station open in the area, with stations in Jaffrey, Peterborough, and other surrounding towns closed. According to store manager Michelle Bishop, the gas lines were unbelievable. She said she witnessed a desperate customer cut in line while another who had been waiting for close to an hour for fuel burst into tears.

An employee from an oil company driving by on one of the first post-storm days saw the madness at the pumps and decided to lend a hand. He drove into the parking lot and got out to direct traffic. Organizing cars into lines and rows, he kept the line moving until almost closing time. Day after day he came in, and still there were lines of dozens of cars.

Generators release deadly carbon monoxide gas, and if they are set up too close to a house, it can seep in, causing a danger to the occupants. Doctor Eric Lasky at Monadnock Community Hospital reported seeing a series of patients come into the hospital who had concerns about carbon monoxide poisoning. Few people died as a result of the ice storm, but most of the fatalities came from carbon monoxide poisoning.

One family that may have narrowly escaped this fate was the family of Amanda Borozinski, a staffer for *The Keene Sentinel* who lives in Rindge. As Amanda wrote in an article for the December 13 edition of the *Sentinel*, she woke up to a strange sound. "I was groggy and disoriented," she wrote. "I rolled over and nudged the form of my sleeping husband. He mumbled an incoherent reply, so I asked again: 'What is that noise?'"

The noised turned out to be the carbon monoxide alarm. After shutting off the alarm and opening the windows, only to have the alarm go off again, Amanda's husband Jake told her they needed to get out of the house as quickly as possible. Her head ached, her throat burned, and her nosed was stuffed. She felt nauseous and confused; she was suffering symptoms of carbon monoxide poisoning. Jake and Amanda fled the house with their 5-year-old son.

Upon inspection, Jake thought their generator could be facing the wrong direction, emitting fumes into the house. Either that or the chimney was blocked with ice, sending wood smoke into the house. Amanda wrote about the severity of the situation. "It hit us both at the same time: We could have died. Six months ago, we didn't even have the carbon monoxide detectors, but because we were going through the adoption process we were required to install them."

Even properly installed generators had their hazards. Terry Varney of Fitzwilliam, New Hampshire, was the victim of generator theft. Due to ice damage from the roads, traffic was rerouted past her house the Sunday after the storm, sending many cars past her brand new generator sitting outside her house. She had gone down to Massachusetts to buy it and had stood in line waiting for a truck shipment like the ones at The Home Depot in Keene. "Nothing has ever been stolen from the property before," Terry said. "We're pretty sure it wasn't a neighbor; it was probably someone who got rerouted. They took it, hookup and all, full of gas. It wasn't running because we thought we'd give it a break. It was on wheels, and full of gas. How handy, huh?"

Some people were not affected at all because their power comes from generators all of the time – people who live off the grid. Ogion Fulford of Guilford, Vermont, lives in a portable, wood-lattice yurt with solar panels that supply his electricity. His water comes from a gravity-fed water source at his neighbor's house. He said that apart from his Internet going down, he was unaffected by the outages. "It's been a way of life for me, appreciating both the environmental issues with it, having a renewable source of power, and appreciating the autonomy that I'll be fine no matter what happens to the grid," Ogion said. "It was a bit of a justification to have the ice storm come and take out the power."

Hardware stores saw the effects of the ice storm even after power had been restored. Rick Edmunds now stocks a generator at his hardware store in Antrim. At The Home Depot, Norm said sales of generators have continued with people preparing for the next big one.

Residents left without electricity beause of the storm eat at the shelter at Wellington Park in Rindge, New Hampshire, on December 19.

Chapter 14
Gimme Shelter

*"People come in, take a shower, have a cup of coffee
and a bowl of soup, then they leave again."*

Debra Harling, Temple, New Hampshire

Whether they kept warm by generator, woodstove, or were shivering under blankets, most of those affected by the ice storm slept in their houses, keeping their pipes from freezing and their basements from flooding. Some took the opportunity to stay with relatives or friends to wait out the aftermath, and a lucky few called hotels before they filled up. For those without those options, however, hundreds of shelters opened in the area of devastation.

Relatively few took advantage of sleeping space that shelters provided. In New Hampshire alone, there were 59 shelters. With more than 400,000 homes without power, peak shelter usage was only 1,254. People came out in droves, however, for the hot meals, temporary warmth, and bottled water the shelters were able to provide. Also, as the lack of electricity and phones increased isolation, shelters became places where neighbors could socialize.

Some shelters opened without a plan, and other towns that had defined shelter plans found they had to scrap them. Lyndeborough, New Hampshire, was in the process of establishing its elementary school as an emergency shelter. In the fall, town workers had installed an emergency generator, but had been unable to get it hooked up because the ground had frozen too quickly. When the ice storm hit, those seeking shelter were directed to nearby Milford.

Principal Nikki McGettigan of the elementary school in Temple, New Hampshire, had the building at her disposal and experience cooking mass meals for nursing homes. She originally thought the storm damage would be cleaned up within 48 hours until she saw the devastation on her way to visit a family member in the hospital. At a faculty Christmas party the Saturday after the storm, it became clear in everyone's mind that school would still be canceled on Monday and beyond.

While at the party, Nikki got a call from someone in town about opening the school as a shelter. After clearing it with the School Administrative Unit, the town of Temple arranged with PSNH to get the elementary school back online as a shelter. Power was restored the next day, and the shelter opened under Nikki's care.

Word of the shelter traveled quickly. Volunteers came out of the woodwork, signing up in droves for three-hour shifts, then actually working for five or six hours at a time. Soon, 100 people were coming in to use the school's one shower every day, standing in line, each holding a towel and a bottle of shampoo. Starting with soups and stews created from food in her own freezer that was in danger of thawing out, Nikki realized that with the volume of people coming in for breakfast, lunch, and dinner, she was going to have to get more creative. All the while, residents came in donating their food.

As Nikki pointed out, the elementary school kitchen is not designed for cooking for large groups. When school is in session, the school lunch is cooked at another location and brought in by truck. Nikki and her staff worked with one oven, which meant she had to use time efficiently. "People started getting their free turkeys from work for Christmas," Nikki said. "I cooked 41 turkeys. From midnight to 6 a.m., I had younger people, college kids, who covered the late night schedule. The nighttime crew had to cook three turkeys every night. We ended up with a big joke here – people say 'Don't forget to brush your teeth' at night and we'd say, 'Don't forget to cook the turkeys.'"

At every meal Nikki and her crew served about 100 people, half of whom were regulars that came three times per day. Firemen, PSNH line workers, police officers, and town officials joined them, eating meals and using the school's phone, one of the few working phones in town for a while. They also used the school as a make-shift emergency command center.

Food was donated, some by the Birchwood Inn up the road, but most by residents who had emptied their freezers. Nikki had to throw some of it away because she could tell it had gone bad, but she made a show of accepting it before secretly tossing it in the trash. She did the best she could to keep the residents' pride intact. "The food was supplied by the same people who were eating," Nikki said. "That way nobody felt like it was a handout; it was just a community supper." Often people would stop in the shelter on their way into town to go shopping somewhere that had power and they would ask Nikki if she needed anything. She would often ask for aluminum foil and other supplies.

Residents stopped in to take showers, get warm, use the wireless Internet, watch TV, talk with their neighbors, eat, and some even got some work done. Nikki set up a special quiet corner for people who usually worked from home to come and use their computers and continue to make a living. The shelter had all kinds of visitors. An egg farmer would bring in fresh eggs every day. Firemen would show up with shivering residents who were trying to sleep in their trucks, or with elderly people who had nowhere else to go.

Several young women from a horse farm showed up exhausted from hauling five-gallon buckets from a pond up to their barn over and over again to keep their 28 horses watered. Some other residents, who were in for a meal, made a few calls and got a generator to hook up to their water pump in the barn. "They were so relieved," Nikki said. "They didn't get water into their house, but at least they had it for their horses."

While Nikki stayed at the shelter, she sent people on their way out the door to put a log on her fire at home to keep her house warm so the pipes would not freeze. She returned to her house only once every two nights to sleep. While she was at the shelter, she stayed awake at all times. People throughout Temple called her efforts heroic.

In Peterborough, Jack Burnett, the executive director of the local chamber of commerce, got a call early in the day after the storm – as many did – from Select Board chairwoman Barbara Miller. She asked him and others to help volunteer at the South Meadow School (SMS) shelter. "It was a network of people in Peterborough," Jack said. "It doesn't have a title, it doesn't have an organizational charter, it doesn't have a bank account, it doesn't have vehicles, but it exists. It's a help web that's out there. When things go wrong on a small or large basis, this informal network mobilizes to deal with it." Jack volunteered at the shelter with his wife and 15-year-old son. His own house in West Peterborough was kept warm by a generator installed to protect 12 tanks of poison dart frogs that his son breeds. As Jack put it, "Humans are a low priority in my house."

As it turned out, the same was true in other households without generators. As the word about the SMS shelter spread, residents started showing up with their pets, asking if they could come in and get warm, too. The Red Cross had rules prohibiting animals in their shelters, but the SMS shelter had not formally become affiliated with the Red Cross; it was just formed on the fly. "It was very much a 'church of what's happening now' shelter," Jack said. "People came and asked, 'Can I come in on a wheelchair?' 'Can I come in and eat and leave?' 'Can I come in and take a shower and leave?' The unofficial motto of the SMS shelter was 'Yes.' Whatever people want, 'Yes.' We'll deal with it."

According to Roland Patten, another community member called by Barbara to volunteer, there was a mix of people in the shelter, but the majority was elderly, and some were on oxygen machines powered by electricity. "That was one of the problems with not having electricity," Roland said. "People needing oxygen were having serious problems."

For the first few days, the SMS shelter ran on generator power. There was only emergency lighting and cold water, but there was heat. The kitchen was electric, so before power was restored, volunteers cooked outside on the porch with gas heaters. Eventually the Red Cross moved in, but rather than allow the organization to take over, Peterborough residents kept partial control over the shelter, continuing to allow pets and doing the best they could to uphold their motto – Yes.

Selectwoman Elizabeth Thomas stayed several nights at the shelter, and she said she would freeze before she would leave her pets. She said the Red Cross tried to move an elderly resident who had an oxygen tank to a nursing home, but the resident did not want to move. The volunteer staff allowed the resident to stay. "The shelter was there right to the end," Elizabeth said. "We said we'd keep it open. The Red Cross took it over for the last couple of days; they said they would keep it open until everyone was safe in their homes and not deport anybody." Elizabeth estimates the SMS shelter housed, fed, or warmed 500 people. PSNH workers came by the shelter for meals, and whenever they did, everyone blew them kisses and brought them their food.

Peggi Brogan, head of the Recreation Department in Rindge, New Hampshire, opened the Rindge shelter Friday evening, December 12, with a generator donated by Park Construction, a company in neighboring Fitzwilliam, which is owned by Rindge residents Steve, Dave, and Mark Norby. The shelter stayed open for 12 days, and according to Peggi's records, volunteers logged 1,342 hours and served 2,150 meals.

As with most of the shelters, few stayed over, but two residents who did were Deborah Idaka and her husband, Yuichi. The first two nights after the storm, the Idakas had stayed at home. As the temperature in their house steadily dropped, they went to Brattleboro, Vermont, which was the closest place where they could find a hotel room. After two nights there, they returned to Rindge and headed to the Recreation Department shelter for another two nights. "That was a fantastic experience," Deborah said. "They have folding doors, so at night they closed the folding doors, and the Red Cross had lent them cots, so if people didn't have a warm place to stay, they could stay there." Deborah watched during the day as people socialized, children played video games together, a woman sewed, and everyone ate. "It felt like this was going to be the future community center of Rindge," she said.

While devastated and without power, many people all over Massachusetts, Maine, Vermont, New Hampshire, New York, and beyond sought refuge in their local shelters. While they encountered fear and frustration, they likewise encountered camaraderie and community.

Rindge, New Hampshire, residents eat beside a decorated Christmas Tree at the shelter at Wellington Park.

A Rutland, Massachusetts, man walks along his ice-covered fence.

Chapter 15
Waiting For Power

"And you just think,
'I don't want to be a pioneer anymore!'"
Debbie Fisher, Spofford, New Hampshire

While many reported that the outages began as a kind of adventure, or a return to a way of life before electricity and running water, few kept the pioneer spirit for long. As one day turned into two days, and two turned into a week, those without power felt their spirits break and their patience wear thin. In Vermont, the outages lasted for five days, and in parts of Maine they lasted six. The 16 counties that were affected in New York State were all back online after eight days. In Massachusetts, except for a few scattered outages, electricity was restored after 12 days.

New Hampshire was hit the hardest, so it was out the longest. And nowhere in New Hampshire was hit harder than the Monadnock region. Power was restored first to the less severely hit northern region of the state, which was back to normal after seven days. Next to come online was the sea coast area, after 10 days. By December 23, day 12 of the restoration effort, the towns with significant numbers of customers left to be restored were Deering, Dublin, Fitzwilliam, Greenfield, Greenville, Hancock, Harrisville, Jaffrey, Mason, New Ipswich, Peterborough, Rindge, Sharon, Temple, and

Ice hangs from a stump in Guilford, Vermont, on December 14.

Troy. Apart from Deering, which is further north, those towns make up the greater Peterborough area.

Marilyn Vose was shocked that it took as long as it did for Peterborough to get electricity. Her first thought when she lost power in her downtown residence was that it would be restored by the end of the day. Why? "…Because it's Peterborough," she said. "It's a centralized location. To me it's the heartbeat of the area." At that, Vose got off relatively easy, spending only seven days without power. But staying with relatives or at hotel rooms wore on her, as did relying on the electricity at work. It wasn't just the lack of electricity; it was a feeling of safety. "You miss being in your own space, your comfort zone," she said. "If I could have stayed here and been warm, I would have been good, but that couldn't happen."

Glenn Coppelman from Kingston, New Hampshire, was out for six days, and he said the novelty wore off after the first. "Once it goes beyond a day or two or three, you find yourself planning your life around keeping the pipes from freezing and keeping the food from spoiling," he said.

In Dublin, Deb Giaimo said she could not even take a shower in a public gym during the 12-day outage at her house. Addled by the constant requirement of keeping warm and keeping hydrated, she became desperate and ill-tempered. She recalled that a woman she knew was shopping in Keene and got blocked into the parking lot

The ice knocked wires knocked off of this house in Cummington, Massachusetts.

by an elderly woman. Deb's friend got very angry with the woman, speaking harshly to her for that small inconvenience. Many reported getting snappy after a few days without power, letting things that normally would slightly annoy blow up into major outbursts. Even a month after having her power restored, Deb had not fully recovered from the draining duration of the outage. She jokingly described the feeling as post-traumatic stress disorder.

One Fitzwilliam woman whose philosophy is to try to live a simpler life got to try that lifestyle out for 10 days. Tracie Smith, a farmer, found herself waking up every three hours to tend to either the woodstove or, eventually, to her generator. Everything she did took much longer than usual, and she thought of pioneers who spent their whole lives on activities required for survival. "They didn't have the time to get involved in all the stuff we get involved in," she said. "They spent most of their lives doing what they needed to."

At the same time, Tracie found herself longing for the modern-day conveniences that before she had fantasized about giving up. She grew to further appreciate hot showers and the quickness of ready heat, water, and food that free up time for other pursuits.

Now, she feels conflicted. She still clings to the idea of a simpler life but understands she also craves the conveniences of modern life. "I don't know if I'd want to trade those opportunities, but I think we're out of control," Tracie said. "Once you experience luxury, though, it's the hardest thing to give it up."

One difficulty for Antrim Town Administrator Neal Cass that was echoed by many officials in small towns was that as the outage went on, the initial burst of volunteers that came out in droves at the beginning began to dwindle. People became burned out or had gotten power back in their homes or had to deal with their own emergencies. "It became more daunting as time went on, how to sort of keep everything going for a longer time," Neal said. "And because you're getting tired, you're just ready for a good night's sleep in your own bed. You started getting into a week and beyond, and volunteers were not able to do some things."

Among the last people to get power back in the Monadnock region were the people living in the shadow of the peak that gives the area its name: Mount Monadnock. Patrick Hummel is the park manager for Monadnock State Park and lives on site. Having become park manager four months earlier, the ice storm became his trial by fire.

Patrick spent 16 days without power. He got reading done and took things day by day. Toward the end of the outage, a friend offered him the use of a generator, but he declined on the grounds that by the time it arrived, it would be more trouble than it was worth. On top of the stress of managing to keep warm was the stress of the work that was to come. Every trail on the mountain was closed due to falling branches, and each would have to be cleared.

While working at the *Ledger-Transcript*, the person I encountered who had been out the longest had lost power for 18 days. Bella Martin, a woman in her mid-80s, endured the outage with her husband of about the same age. They never left home, even after their generator caused a surge, blowing out their light bulbs. "We stuck it out in good order," she told me later. Having lived out west riding horses as a younger woman, she wanted to be a cowboy. Cowboys don't feel pain, she said, so she would never complain about anything. Mother Nature gave her over two weeks of potential complaints, but in her words, "You just need to have the pioneer spirit."

Town officials and others checking the welfare of elderly residents reported a pattern: Elderly folks in general coped better, remembering a time before the constant dependence on electricity.

One such trick from that time was taught to 26-year-old Henry Bley-Vroman by his grandmother, with whom he was living in Alstead. In order to keep warm at night, both normally used electric blankets, which did not work during the aftermath of the ice storm. Instead, they heated brick-sized soap stones in their wood stove and tucked under the blankets at night. "That was incredible," Henry said. "It was far more effective and pleasant than electric blankets. You wrap them up in towels and push them off to the side. It's like having another warm body in bed with you, except you're snuggling with a soap stone block."

Doris "Granny D" Haddock is a 99-year-old activist and Dublin resident famous for walking coast-to-coast across America in support of campaign-finance reform. It was an activity she began at the age of 88 and finished at 90. While she has lived for nearly a century, the only comparison she had for the 2008 ice storm happened 70 years earlier when she was housebound for a week with two small children. "The hurricane of 1938; that's the only other real storm that I ever encountered in all my 99 years," Granny D said. "This is a very unusual thing that happened." Granny D spent the first week of the ice storm waiting it out in Massachusetts, where she had just completed a speaking engagement, and spent a few more days in Keene before she was able to return home.

While the wait was long, help finally did arrive. Utility workers stretched to their limits made the rounds and eventually got people back online, working day in and day out. Of all those affected by the storm, even those out for the longest period of time, most agreed that utility workers had the toughest job of all.

A Public Service of New Hampshire truck in Candia, New Hampshire, on December 15.

Act IV
An Unprecedented Restoration

*A man in a bucket works on trees and wires in Worcester,
Massachusetts, on December 15.*

Chapter 16
The Toughest Job of All

"The largest challenges are simply getting to the areas
that need help and also the sheer number of those areas."
Martin Murray, spokesman,
Public Service of New Hampshire

Two months after the storm, Public Service of New Hampshire released a report about the ice storm titled "Record Outage, Record Recovery." As the largest provider of electricity in New Hampshire, PSNH also had the largest number of outages to repair – 322,000 homes all told, more than half of its customers. According to the U.S. Census taken in 2000, households in New Hampshire numbered just under 475,000 that year.

The numbers alone give an idea of the scale of the restoration for PSNH. The company replaced 1,300 transformers, installed 13,600 fuses, replaced 780 utility poles and restrung 105 miles of wire. Customer service representatives fielded more than 408,000 calls. There were 1,700 employees and retirees called into duty, and 1,205 crews from in state and out working at the peak of the process. By Christmas Eve, 13 days after the ice storm, the electricity service of 99.9 percent of customers had been restored. The cost was $75 million. In its 82 years of existence, the largest number of PSNH outages previously had been 93,000, less than a third of the outages from the 2008 storm.

Wires pushed into snow banks by plow trucks remain by the side of the road in Nelson, New Hampshire, nearly two months after the storm.

As shocking as some of those numbers are, the one I found the most surprising was the 14- to 17-hour work day PSNH employees endured. Of all the people without electricity struggling to keep their houses and families warm, PSNH Chief Operating Officer Gary Long said his heart went out to the utility employees and their families the most. Not only were they working extremely hard, but often their families were dealing with the results of outages at home.

Halfway through the restoration effort, I spoke with Jaffrey resident and PSNH employee Dave Letourneau. The only time he had available to talk was at 5:30 in the morning, so that's the time I interviewed him. Working from 6 in the morning to 11 at night, Dave was rarely able to see his 13-year-old son and his wife, who kept the fires going at the house to keep it warm. His other son, 23-year-old Josh, worked his own 17-hour shift in nearby New Ipswich.

Dave started work early on the morning after the storm, trying to remove a tree from Old Peterborough Road in Jaffrey while trees were falling all around. It was a dangerous situation, but no one on his crew was injured. Safety was always at the forefront of his thinking, especially with the adverse weather conditions. During the weeks of restoration, there were two more major snowstorms. Besides working in the difficult conditions, some plow trucks would unknowingly push downed lines under snow banks as they cleared the roads, slowing the linemen even further. "When it's going to snow as hard as it is, we slow it down," Dave said. "Slow and steady and safe wins the race. We just keep plugging away at it."

Tensions mounted as the effort to restore electricity continued. There were many incidents in which one house would get its power back while the house next door would have to wait several more days. The protocol for fixing lines was based on the number of people each repair would impact. If there was a choice between fixing a break that would restore 200 people and one that would restore five, of course the linemen would be sent to the break affecting the 200, often making it appear as though they were leaving some jobs unfinished. Many customers did not understand this and complained, but for the most part they were very grateful for the work the linemen did.

The work was exhausting, but rewarding. The things that kept

Jacob Trudelle from Marlow, New Hampshire, worked as a tree-trimmer for 17-hour shifts while his family stayed home with their battery powered wood pellet stove.

Utility workers repair wires on Route 9 in Vermont between Brattleboro and Marlboro on December 14.

Dave going through the ordeal personally were hearing children cheering as their power came back and people saying "Thank you." There was also the commitment to the work of a utility employee. "We're in the business of keeping the lights going; that's what we're paid for," Dave said. "Some people take electricity for granted, but it takes people to keep it going."

PSNH released a series of videos on YouTube about the restoration effort, in which Gary Long and other employees discussed what conditions were like. Among those interviewed was Supervising Communication and Transmission Control worker Johnathan Wottrich. Talking as snow fell around him, Johnathan said he hoped for just a couple of inches rather than the six to eight the weathermen predicted, and which eventually fell. At the time the video was made the difficulties seemed unending. "You start driving down these roads and you see wires up, and you think 'Well, that's okay,' but then you drive further down the road and there are four or five sections lying down on the ground," Johnathan said.

Tim Rourkey of the PSNH central supply warehouse in Bow, New Hampshire, said the warehouse doubled its staff hours to stay open day and night. In the company's history, there had never been a larger re-supply effort, with a year's worth of materials used in four days.

Line crews worked around the clock, with some taking on the night shift, using spotlights to see what they were doing. Steve Anderson was interviewed as the working nightshift foreman in Candia, New Hampshire. His crew worked as others slept, and they worked the same 17 hours as the day crews. "We'll go to sleep at 7, and while we're sleeping there are other crews working," Steve said. "They're on a swing shift so at all times there are crews working. We just go around the clock."

The response from subscribers was tremendous, according to Steve. He said his crew was offered food, coffee, and other drinks. Gestures like that were greatly welcomed after such long hours. "It's nice to see that these people appreciate what we do and it just keeps us going basically," Steve said. "It's a great job where you can actually help out your community and help these people get back to a normal lifestyle."

A temporary Public Service of New Hampshire work center in Fitzwilliam, New Hampshire.

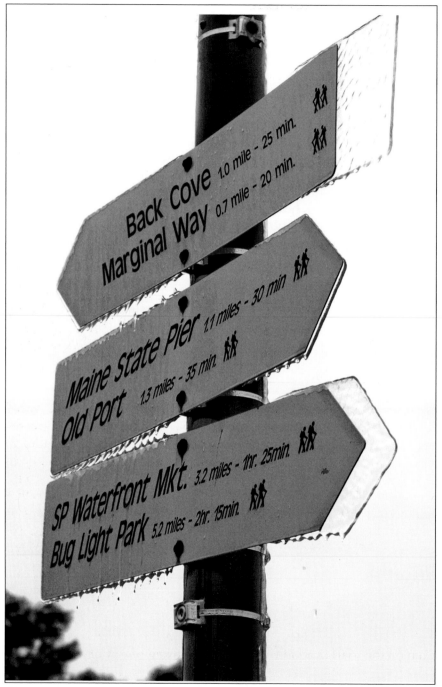

Signs covered in ice in Wells, Maine, on December 12.

A Public Service of New Hampshire employee works on a utility pole in Candia, New Hampshire, on December 15.

Supporting PSNH was the New Hampshire Army National Guard, which for the first time ever was called to assist in power restoration. Its largest single mission was to support the utility in order to protect the public and get power restored as quickly as possible. Greg Crotto, a command sergeant-major in the guard, used to work for PSNH. He compared the damage to a tornado that had come through central New Hampshire five months earlier but said to multiply it 100-fold. "I don't think anybody can visualize the amount of work that the utilities across this state have suffered and the amount of work that goes into it," Greg said. "Seeing guys working out there 16-hour days in the cold – and it's cold out there – it gives you a different appreciation, even for me having worked there 33 years."

Tree trimming crews and phone service workers joined the linemen on the roads and in the air. They worked one after another, first tree trimmers, then electricity workers, and finally, phone crews. Everybody worked overtime.

Jacob Trudelle, a tree-trimmer for Asplundh Tree Expert Com-

Public Service of New Hampshire line crews in New Hampshire on December 15.

Public Service of New Hampshire wire repairs in Candia, New Hampshire, on December 15.

A Public Service of New Hampshire lineman moves a branch off of a wire on December 15.

A Public Service of New Hampshire crew works through a blizzard in Wilton, New Hampshire, on December 20.

pany, was called by his boss at 4 a.m. at his house in Marlow, New Hampshire. Working the same 6 a.m. to 11 p.m. shift Dave worked for PSNH, Jacob said his wife and kids were asleep when he left and asleep when he came home. They had a pellet stove with a battery backup, so they were able to keep the house warm while he was away. The early hour and the falling trees made working that morning a tiring and frightening prospect for Jacob, but he quickly adjusted. A tree trimming veteran of 11 years, Jacob had a lot of experience clearing the roads and lines, though never as extreme as following the December ice storm.

Thane Page worked for FairPoint Communications, which had recently purchased a lot of the rural infrastructure in Maine, New Hampshire, and Vermont. The way he described his worksite, "everything was white and broken." He worked at least 12 hours a day after the storm hit. Between Thanksgiving and the new year, the only day off he got was Christmas Day. "It was harder than normal, but you know it's just something you've got to do," Thane said.

Thane's home in Swanzey, New Hampshire, had power after the storm; it flickered out for only a few minutes on December 11. But many of Thane's coworkers did their jobs without electricity at home. It could not have been easy, Thane said, but the workers beside him didn't show the signs of the extra stress that Thane was sure was there.

The day after Christmas, a thank you message to Public Service of New Hampshire at Club Cannon in Peterborough, New Hampshire, could be seen.

Thane began working for the phone company the year of the 1998 ice storm, so he had some experience working through difficult situations. As with the power and tree crews, safety was always on his mind. "You've got to make your own decisions to be safe," Thane said. "The conditions warranted extra caution."

While local line workers were stretched to their limits in the early parts of the restoration, PSNH and other power companies brought workers from places as far away as Maryland, Ohio, and Canada to come and fix the damaged wires. For many New Hampshire natives, those out-of-towners were a welcome site. Others found some of them incompetent or unknowledgeable about working in local conditions.

Ron Reed of Stoddard said he had mixed experiences with crews from out of the area. One truck with an out-of-state license plate ran a stop sign and blocked a nearby road for no reason he could see, and he was unable to pass. He said others had a similar impression of the crews from far away. A friend of his from Troy, in a neighborhood that was in the process of coming back online, came home to find an out-of-state utility service truck parked on his road. He offered them coffee or sandwiches, which they refused with a brusque tone of voice. Two hours later, Ron's friend looked out the window to see the workers still sitting inside their truck, not having done anything.

While the crew sat in the truck, a big Canadian truck arrived, and out strode one man alone. Standing six-and-a-half feet tall, he wore only a sweatshirt and bib overalls against the cold. Walking past the other truck of shivering service workers, the Canadian dragged over some wires and fiddled with the connections. In 20 minutes, the lights flickered, and came back on. "Them boys knew how to take care of the trouble stuff," he said of the Canadians.

As the crews worked in the fields, the PSNH Communications Department sent out updates using the Internet as many as six times per day. Using their psnhnews.com site and twitter.com, a Web site devoted to allowing its users to post quick messages, they dispersed information including how many outages remained, how many crews were working, where the crews were directed to work, which towns still required assistance, and when those towns

A caravan of utility trucks in Readsboro, Vermont, on December 16.

could expect to be worked on. While seeing those updates became a challenge for those without electricity or Internet service, news organizations published them, and some people were able to check them on mobile phones.

But misinformation still spread. In Durham, New Hampshire, Jan Heirtzler and her family were told by town officials that they would have to cut their phone line at their house so that cables could be removed from the road for snow plows coming through. When power crews came to reconnect Jan's neighbors, they were unable to turn her family's power back on because of the cut at her house. They called PSNH to find out what they should do. "We were told by a representative, who we later found was from Connecticut, that it was our responsibility to remount the meter box, which had been torn off the house, and it was probably that which kept our power from being reconnected," Jan explained. "I immediately called an electrician to have that done, only to find the next day, after it had been remounted, that this was required only in Connecticut, and that crews would have remounted the box as a matter of course. PSNH still owes us $75 for that."

In the Peterborough area, where the damage was the most severe, PSNH normally has three trucks assigned to the district. By the time the restoration in that area was in full swing, there were 400. PSNH set up substations at the Army National Guard Armory in Peterborough, Boynton Middle School in New Ipswich, and the Park Construction facility in Fitzwilliam.

The company directed its workers from a centralized office, attempting to coordinate relief efforts so that everyone could finish as quickly as possible. But on the ground, the non-local crews needed local guides to show them where certain roads were and how to get from one place to another in the most efficient way. Roland Patten, who had been in business for 40 years in Peterborough and knew most of the local roads, agreed to be one such guide.

Roland rode along with three different crews during the restoration effort, one from Maine, one from Vermont, and one from Raymond, New Hampshire. The crews to which he was assigned worked on digging holes in the ground for replacement utility poles. As he directed the crews, Roland got a chance to see some of the most devastated areas firsthand and assess the damage for himself. "It was pretty daunting," Roland said. "I was impressed with how fast they could do an area where there was a lot of damage because it just seemed to me that there was an amazing amount of work."

The large groups of trucks were unmistakable to those without power. As those armadas moved from street to street, friends and neighbors declared to one another that help was on the way. Restaurant owners fed these large groups en masse, charging company credit cards for the enormous amounts of food for hundreds of workers. At the substation in the Peterborough Armory, the workers were fed by Tony Reagan of Bowling Acres, who moved his kitchen operation to Peterborough's ConVal High School with PSNH's help so he could serve more people.

In the months following the restoration, information beyond the report released by PSNH was difficult to get because of an ongoing investigation into the company's response to the storm. The latest information I received was that lawyers advised employees not to discuss the restoration through the month of August.

The restoration effort will not be soon forgotten by company employees or by the people of New Hampshire, whose bills will wind up serving as a reminder over the next several years. Of the $75 million the event cost the company, only $25 million was covered by savings and insurance. The remaining $50 million will be passed on to the customer.

Sunlight shines on a solar panel in Guilford, Vermont.

Chapter 17
Getting it Back:
Let There Be Light

*"It was amazing to get power back. We were just starting
to realize how much we are used to the conveniences,
and then one hour later, it went out again."*
M'lue Zahner, Harrisville, New Hampshire

Ask people who lost power during the ice storm to talk about the moment their power was restored and they will be able to tell you exactly what it was like. While much of the storm and its aftermath included whole days people would probably rather forget, getting electricity back was an experience many compared to winning the lottery.

After five days without power, John Matesowicz saw a house on his road in Gardner, Massachusetts, with the lights on while driving home his daughters, 9-year-old Zaylie and 4-year-old Skyla. Dismissing the thought that electricity had been restored, he assumed the house must have a newly purchased generator. Rolling up to his own house, however, he saw the automatic porch light turned on.

The power was back, and when he realized he and his family wouldn't have to spend another night camping in their own home, he joyously "flipped out." "I came into the house and my little ca-

A utility truck makes its way down a Kennebunk, Maine, street on December 12.

ble box light was on. I started screaming," he said. "I cranked the thermostat, plugged everything back in, turned on my computer. My kids were completely flipping out. They had gone without TV and Nickelodeon for five days. They were sitting there so happy they had power. It was one of the nicest feelings." John spent the rest of the day calling everyone he knew. The intensity of his thrill getting electricity back rivaled the dismay he felt discovering his car smashed by a tree right after the storm. Having run out of food a few days earlier, he was able to shop and cook a real meal with meat, potatoes, and vegetables, and there was light to cook by as well. Power was freedom, and his sentence was up.

Getting the power back also helped with other aspects of recovery. John and his neighbors had been attempting to clear debris with handsaws, and now they were able to plug in chainsaws.

After only five days without power, John couldn't help but feel lucky with so many others still without. His next-door neighbor had to wait an additional four days after John got his power. Early into the recovery, he had heard stories of people living on back roads getting notices that they would have to wait 30 days to get their power restored.

Neal Cass, the town administrator for Antrim, got to experience the thrill of getting power back twice. The first was after two days when the Antrim Town Office got its power restored, and the second was a few days later when he got power back at his Hancock home. Apart from Main Street, most of Antrim was still without power, but he knew that at least his own family was warm. "I'm not sure I could describe it," Neal said. "You're just so excited. We were just like – 'Finally!'"

And as power began to be restored, "power envy" set in. People passed lights on their road and utility trucks working on their neighbors' houses, only to come home to darkness. It was more than Deb Giaimo of Dublin, New Hampshire, could stand. She was out for 12 days, among the longest in the region, which she described as "11 days too long." Houses one quarter of a mile down the road from her got their power restored a full three days earlier than hers. And the fact that power was so tantalizingly close only made living without it harder. "The sense of frustration bordered on desperation," Deb said. "You think, 'Why can't you come in and finish doing the lines on this stretch of road?'"

Each day, Deb would ask herself, "Is this the day?," and when it finally came, the reaction was "Why couldn't this have been done before?" She realized that it was a hard job being out there restoring the lines, but she couldn't help feeling some antipathy for the line

A house in Mechanicville, New York, viewed through ice- and snow-covered branches on December 13.

workers mixed with appreciation for the difficulty of the work. Being without power so long brought out in her the negative qualities we all usually keep buried.

One Milford, New Hampshire, resident decided not to tell anyone she had gotten power back after two days. She was too ashamed because those around her were out for so much longer.

For most, however, getting it back was a communal experience. In Nelson, New Hampshire, Lisa Sieverts and Max Nunnemaker shared a kiss under their newly lit porch light after 12 days living without. At the Temple Elementary School shelter, people who had gotten their power back would call the shelter, letting others who were there know. Everyone eating meals and helping out would cheer for them. Beth Krommes, a Peterborough children's book illustrator, celebrated by screaming in joy with her family. One of her daughters found she did miss the candlelight, however, which she thought was nicer than the electric light. Beth went on the next month to win the prestigious Caldecott Medal for a book coincidentally dealing with the subject of light and dark, called *The House in the Night*.

Working at her parents' laundromat in Keene, New Hampshire, Melissa Lee heard from her mother when power was restored at their house in Westmoreland. Her mother could hardly form sentences trying to tell her what had happened, using the phone for the first time in nearly three days. Immediately, her parents started flushing the toilets and filling the bathtubs with water in case the power went out again. The power did flicker and go out twice more for periods of a few hours before it was finally fully restored.

In Camphill Village in Copake, New York, Tali Fridman's power flickered and was restored, only to be lost again. People in the village rejoiced only to be plunged back into confusion and darkness. "When the power came back, I was between the kitchen and the living room and I don't even remember what first came on," Tali said. "There was applauding and hurrahing, and supper was set out." Tali was surprised how quickly everyone got back into a routine when power was restored after being thrown into disarray. By the next day, almost everything was back to normal.

A firefighter, a landlord, a business owner, and a parent in Harrisville, New Hampshire, Steve Weber had to take care of a great variety of tasks when the power went out. Between checking on houses, bringing wood to his tenants, keeping his own house warm, and clearing the roads, it was welcome news when a PSNH truck crew

Pam Crook stands in front of her blocked road in Greenfield, New Hampshire, on December 12.

Don Primrose stands beside his plow truck at his property in Sullivan, New Hampshire.

informed him he should have power later that day. But the power did not come back on when he flipped on his lights. Despondent, Steve hooked his generator back up to the house for another night. By the next day, PSNH had indeed repaired the line. "It was a huge let down and then really good," Steve said. "It made us appreciate having power and the luxury of it – how much we're dependent on it."

The unconscious expectation of having lights coming on after flipping a switch stayed with people even as power outages continued into multiple weeks. Many flipped switches automatically when entering a dark room. For at least one man, however, that habit was how he found out power had been restored. Don Primrose was doing chores in his barn in Sullivan, New Hampshire, and threw down some hay to flip the light switch after 12 days without power. "I just thought, 'You idiot, there's no power,' but then the lights came on," he said. Thanking the nearby crew that turned the lights on, he learned they were from Texas and had never seen snow before.

At Peterborough's MacDowell Colony, the campus power came back slowly, building by building. Alexandra Gardner, stuck at the colony because a tree had flattened her car, said people would get excited as the power got closer and closer to the artist studios, where the artists would be able to do work again. More important, however, was when power was restored to a building with full bathroom facilities and everyone could take showers.

Toward the end of the restoration, only houses that were particularly difficult to reach remained without power, and trucks came in groups to restore them. One public works director said he saw four trucks working all day on one driveway to restore power to one house. Greenfield, New Hampshire, resident Pam Crook said she could tell the day she was going to get her power back. "We saw them coming down the road," she said. "It wasn't one truck; it was five trucks. 'That's it,' I said. 'We're going to get power.'"

Emergency management officials uniformly called the outages an inconvenience more than anything else, but being an inconvenience of duration, the most common reaction to the power returning was one of great relief. Bill Burt, manager of Little Roy's convenience store in Peterborough, summed up his feelings of returning to the way things were. "I could get to work at my regular time, and take a hot shower when I wanted to," he said. "That was pretty much it – getting that sense of normalcy back. The routine of life is a comfort, knowing that there's a hot shower, a warm bed, a chance to go to work and interact with my customers again."

But even with power restored the effects of the ice storm lingered, with clean-up and catch-up, not to mention the looming Christmas holiday, which for some was the greatest inconvenience of all. Getting power back may have been a relief, but life couldn't return to normal yet with the holidays just around the corner.

Scott Oliver hangs Christmas decorations on an evergreen tree that fell on his roof in Harrisville, New Hampshire, during the storm. The tree and the decorations stayed in place through the New Year.

Chapter 18
The Ice Storm that Stole Christmas

"I put the decorations away. It was not the same as it normally would be. If it wasn't for the grandkids coming over, we wouldn't have had Christmas."
Patti Hills, New Ipswich, New Hampshire

Marilyn Vose of Peterborough described getting power back as a feeling "better than Christmas." For many, however, electricity literally was restored on Christmas, or it was close enough that there was no time to shop, decorate a tree, or celebrate the way that they were used to. Some canceled Christmas, or at least put it off. Others made Christmas a joyful end to the ice storm outages, which added to the celebration of power's restoration.

For Rebecca Karam of Ashby, Massachusetts, the Christmas of 2008 was set to be even more special than most. Rebecca was pregnant, and her due date was December 28. Before the ice storm, her only thought was that she wanted the baby to come before Christmas, an early present.

All that changed when the ice storm hit on December 11. She was in her 37th week and decided with her husband Tony and 10-year-old son Cameron to head to her parents house in Pepperell, Massachusetts, half an hour away. Her parents had no power either, but at least they had a woodstove and a generator. In Rebecca's mind, the outage would last only a few days and then her family would

Conifer trees are covered with ice rather than decorations on Pinnacle Mountain in Lyndeborough, New Hampshire.

be able to return home. Instead, their power was out for 12 days. The final days of her dream pregnancy to end on Christmas were turning into a nightmare. "It was very frustrating," Rebecca said. "It was packing up our whole life and moving out. I continued to work as did my husband, but my whole routine was totally off, and I was trying to prepare for the new baby."

While the family holed up in Pepperell, their house in Ashby weathered the elements. Rebecca's husband attempted to drain the pipes, but there was no way to blow the pipes out. He did a gravity drain, but that left some water in the pipes. When the power finally came back on two days before Christmas, the furnace would not start and the pipes were frozen. When they were able to assess what was wrong, they found 12 breaks in their pipes caused by ice.

The leaking water caused massive damage to the baby's room, which Rebecca and her husband had meticulously prepared. The baby's closet had been destroyed, the carpet was ruined, and all of the clothing waiting for her was wet, along with the blankets, sheets, and all of the gifts she had gotten for the baby from family and friends. Worst of all, a baptismal gown, which had been in the family since Rebecca's great grandfather's birth, was ruined. Most recently, it had been worn by Cameron. "The last straw was in the baby's room when we opened the closet and there were inches of water on the floor," Rebecca said. "I was in tears. My brother kept saying, 'No crying, no crying.' I couldn't hold it back anymore; I was so drained by this. I cried for two hours in front of the heating guy. I felt bad for him."

While cleaning up the house, ripping up the carpets, and sending clothes to the dry cleaners, Rebecca and Tony wanted Cameron to have as normal a Christmas as they could provide. Stressed about the holiday and about her pregnancy, Rebecca told her boss what she was going through and got some comfort. "She told me my baby would wait for everything to be calm," she said. "I remember thinking, 'Please, baby, please don't come early.'"

And yes, when Christmas morning came, it was like… Christmas morning. Cameron was home and having Christmas just like Rebecca wanted him to. After celebrating for the whole day, Rebecca went into labor Christmas night. Her healthy baby arrived early on December 26. "Her name is Madelyn, and she's absolutely perfect," Rebecca said. "All the distress of that time, I guess it didn't really affect Madelyn because she's perfect. We were so happy that I didn't even think about it until I came back home and remembered we still had a lot of work ahead of us."

Christmas lights and icicles both hang in front of this sign in Portland, Maine, on December 12.

In the months that followed, Madelyn slept in her parents' room. Rebecca and Tony had to negotiate with the insurance companies to try to get coverage for the damage. Walls were repainted, carpeting was replaced, and through it all, it was the late Christmas present that made the ordeal bearable. "It was pretty poor timing, but my boss was right. My baby did wait for things to calm down. The baby came and made everything worth all that work."

The Christmas season helped others persevere during the storm. Scott Oliver, owner of the historic Harrisville Inn, found an 80-foot tree lying across the roof on the day after the storm. It could have been worse – much worse – so rather than get upset about the cracked plaster and considerable expense of having the tree removed, Scott brought out his Christmas decorations and put them on the pine tree lying across his roof. It stayed on the inn through the New Year and turned out to be a big hit.

Many decided to postpone Christmas, or not to celebrate it at all. The stresses of not having power for various amounts of time during those two preceding weeks discouraged people from shopping and decorating. Among the worst off were line workers. In the laundromat in Keene, Melissa Lee tried to console a worker bringing clothes in for his crew. He was close to tears because he was from Maryland and might not make it home to his family for Christmas.

"It was a terrible time of year to have a disaster, the two or three weeks before Christmas," Peterborough Public Works Director Rodney Bartlett said. Rodney worked closely with workers from PSNH as they restored the town. As the holiday approached, Town Administrator Pam Brenner had a tree sent down to the armory, where the line workers had set up a base of operations. Greatly appreciating that gesture, the PSNH workers put a sign on the tree the next day that said "Everybody home by Christmas."

The desire to finish the work before the holiday was on everyone's mind. Christmas became the deadline for the power companies, for the sake of customers and workers alike. "By the time of the 24th, 99 percent of all the people were back with power throughout the region," Rodney said. "That holiday kept everyone trying to get power back focused on getting it done." Even with that impressive statistic, there were still people out at Christmas and there were still line crews working to restore them.

At Temple Elementary School's shelter, Principal Nikki McGettigan and her staff of volunteers decided on Christmas Eve to hold

Christmas dinner at the shelter as a closing celebration the next night. One contractor with PSNH, D'Orsey DeWispelaere from Milford, New Hampshire, wrote a letter to the *Ledger-Transcript* about that final supper, which was printed on January 15. What follows is an excerpt:

"I ended my shift on the afternoon of Christmas Eve. I was tired and overwhelmed, thinking what was I going to do for my family's Christmas dinner? Well, the fantastic people of Temple were prepared to feed everyone on Christmas day and I accepted their invitation to return for Christmas dinner. My family and I were warmly welcomed. There was great food and residents were playing festive music on violins and keyboards. Thank you, Temple residents. Your community is full of many wonderful people."

In some cases, the Christmas spirit prevailed, but it was a rare exception that allowed for Christmas shopping, especially in the heavily impacted Monadnock region. In New Hampshire, estimated damage for businesses was more than $13 million, according to the state's Division of Economic Development. Communications and Legislative Director Steve Boucher explained, "It was almost all loss of income. There was very little physical damage. That was very much the exception rather than the rule."

Businesses went into price-slashing mode to recover, discounting items well beyond what they would have before the storm. Companies that rely on the Christmas season were particularly susceptible, and that includes many small and family businesses prevalent in the Monadnock region. Of the reported damages, nearly all of it, $10,599,302, came from Cheshire and Hillsborough counties, which include the Monadnock region. Many New Hampshire businesses sought short-term loans and financing provided through the state. Others looked into making more energy-efficient choices to save money.

Top officials from the Peterborough Chamber of Commerce said conditions were dicey for many of their members. Chamber Associate Director Pam Crook said the priority to buy presents just was not there following the storm. Then, when Christmas passed, there was no need. "The time had come and gone," Pam said. "It was a tragic loss that way."

In order to recoup damages, some Peterborough businesses got together to organize a sales event in January. Camelia Sousa of the Sharon Arts Center in downtown Peterborough was involved. "It was a good response," she said. "It didn't recoup all of the damages, but it was nice to see people out and about around town. January is a slow time in Depot Square, and it felt busier. The weather helped to bring people out."

A few months later, in response to the ice storm and an economic downturn occurring at the same time, the Sharon Arts Center, a pillar of the Peterborough arts community, temporarily closed its downtown exhibition gallery, in many ways the most visible part of the business.

In Windham, New Hampshire, Donna Robertson's coffee shop and gift business struggled through the Christmas season. Usually, Donna keeps five people on staff during the month of December, and after the ice storm, she tried to get by with two. Business during December accounts for 40 percent of her sales.

Eventually, as power returned, customers did as well, and the final push before Christmas was profitable. But Donna herself never got up her own tree. "Normally we deck out for Christmas, but I was at a point where I was like, I can't even deal," Donna said. "You could sense that people were behind schedule. They just wanted Christmas to come and be over with."

In addition to Christmas, the Jewish holiday Chanukah was affected by the outages. Normally a "festival of lights," many were still without power on the first night of the eight-day holiday on December 21. Jewish families had another reason to light candles on those nights, a habit that for many had become routine.

Nelson, New Hampshire, home to one of the longest-running American contra dance series – more than 200 years – had to make a rare cancellation on the Monday after the storm. Normally, the dance happens every Monday year round, rain, shine, or otherwise. But the Nelson Town Hall, where the dance takes place, did not have power. For the dance's organizers, that made it extra important to have the yearly solstice and Christmas night dances.

Don Primrose of neighboring Sullivan was upset at the decision to cancel. A weekly caller at the Monday dances, Don's phone did not work, and he did not get word until shortly before the dance was to begin. "It was a place of community," he said. "It might have been only an hour or an hour-and-a-half long. We abandoned them that night."

The solstice and subsequent Christmas dances did happen, the solstice with a generator and the Christmas dance with newly restored power. At the dance on Christmas day, the feeling among participants was one of joy that they had made it through the ordeal. Just the day before, PSNH trucks decked out in Christmas lights came through town, restoring the power. Dance organizer Lisa Sieverts, with Max Nunnemaker, sang a song at the dance by Nelson residents Laurie Redfern Smith and Jonathan Smith. Set to the tune of the "12 Days of Christmas," the song was called "The 12 Days Without Power." It was dedicated to "Our newest heroes: the Men in Buckets." Dancers sang along as they proceeded through the song. The final verse is included here:

On the twelfth day without power, my true love said to me,
"What, another blizzard!!!"
"What, a blizzard!!!"
"How do we do these dishes?"
"I stoked the fire LAST time"
"Something somewhere smells bad"
"It's your turn to fill the woodbox"
"You need a shower"
"I CAN'T FIND MY HEADLAMP"
"Better haul some water"
"Glad we have a woodstove"
"Let's dine by candlelight"
"Or get a pizza and see a movie."

With power restored and Christmas done, the final chapter of the ice storm epic became an epic itself: the clean up. The Christmas tree was just the first of many trees to be disposed of.

Four weeks after the ice storm, a large branch still dangles from a power cable in Peterborough, New Hampshire.

ACT V
THE MONTHS THAT FOLLOWED

A Monadnock State Park trail crew, including Park Manager Patrick Hummel (left) prepares to clear the way up the mountain.

Chapter 19
Spring Cleaning

---

*"It still looks like a war zone. We still have
trees out back with huge branches off of them.
You can still see the mess."*
Elizabeth Williams, Nelson, New Hampshire, 5 months after the storm

---

Outages stretched on for weeks after the storm, but even after power was restored, cleanup and recovery took months. As 2008 turned to 2009, "to do" lists replaced New Year's resolutions as people realized what was ahead of them: projects delayed by and resulting from the ice storm. They braced themselves for the spring thaw, revealing the trunks, limbs, branches, and other debris brought down by the storm. It was apparent to all that some of the storm's effects would last for years, and the impression it left would remain for lifetimes.

The first order of business was getting the kids back to school. After 25 days without classes in the Monadnock region, even the students were ready to return to the classroom. Jessica Hargrove, a high school junior from Wilton, summed up the feelings of many when she spoke to me a few days before students were set to finally return to school on Monday, January 5. "It was good at first because we didn't have to get up in the morning, didn't have to do homework," she said. "But after being out of school for so long,

On April 17, more than four months after the storm, debris is still piled by the side of the road in New Ipswich, New Hampshire.

I'm bored. I need something to do." Like most in the region, Jessica spent a fair amount of her "vacation" without power. Passing the time playing board games with her younger brother, reading books, drawing, and doing some chores around the house, she was definitely ready to return to classes to see her friends and teachers, even if it did mean falling back into the dreaded routine of rising early and doing homework at night.

In a cruel joke on area school districts, however, a smaller ice storm swept through the region that Monday morning, delaying school for two hours and canceling morning kindergarten. Two days later, on Wednesday, yet another storm closed schools for the whole day, bringing school district snow day totals into double digits just a week into January, 2009.

In the months that followed, school boards met to determine what was to be done to make up the lost time. Would graduations have to be pushed back two weeks? Would students have to attend classes on Saturdays or during February and April vacations? Could districts extend the school day to make up some of the time? This was the most severe situation involving missed classes that these school boards had ever encountered, and in typical New Hampshire "Live Free or Die" fashion, the make-up decisions were left to each local district.

Education Commissioner Lyonel Tracy did give officials an attractive option, however, citing a state law allowing districts to request a waiver of the 180-day requirement in case of weather or other emergencies. About a week after the ice storm, the commissioner sent out a communication naming waivers as a viable make-up alternative. "After a superintendent and the school board consider available alternatives, as commissioner, I will be very willing to consider requests for a waiver," he wrote.

Another law New Hampshire districts were able to use to their advantage was one approved the year before, allowing them to choose whether to count instructional time by the traditional 180-day requirement or institute a new hour-based requirement. The new law mandated 990 hours of instructional time per year for high

Debris sits by the side of the road in Worcester, Massachusetts, on December 16.

school and middle school students and 945 hours for elementary school students. The 180-day schedule most districts were still using provided quite a few more than the 990 hour minimum (180 times a roughly six hour school day is 1,080 hours), and some districts applied to be hour districts rather than day districts following the storm.

This strategy was particularly popular in the Monadnock region.

In the Jaffrey-Rindge Cooperative School District, the school board originally planned to require school attendance for three days during April vacation, but changed its mind after hearing from parents who already planned trips for that time. Instead, they opted to extend the school day for 30 minutes into the afternoon in the months of February through April. Between this and holding classes on two teacher workshop days, the district held its last day of school on June 19, with graduation still occurring on June 12 as planned before the storm.

The neighboring Mascenic District in New Ipswich also extended the school day, adding 10 minutes to both the beginning and end. To make up the rest of the time, officials applied for and received a waiver from the state. Peterborough's ConVal District also received a state waiver for some of the days and extended its school year later into June.

As far as some educators were concerned, the missed days were gone forever. I spoke with fourth grade Peterborough Elementary teacher Sue Kretchman as she was getting her room ready for the returning students after the long winter break. The school board had not yet made up its mind about what to do, but Sue said that in some ways it did not matter. "It's making it up," she said. "It's not equivalent to the time you lost." Months later, in May, I caught up with Sue to ask how her class was doing. She said the class was behind where she hoped it would be, particularly in science and math.

The ice storm had other school-related effects beyond academics. Jaffrey-Rindge's Conant High School boys' basketball team, which had a 63-game winning streak spanning three seasons, lost the first game it played after students returned from the 25-day hiatus. And at Mascenic High School, for the first time in several years, no students submitted work to the New Hampshire Scholastic Art Awards as a result of the deadline coming up too soon after the ice storm.

Over the next several months, teachers worked to cram all the curriculum they could into the time they had left in the school year. Peterborough Elementary Principal Susan Copley said in mid-February that teachers were trying to get students back up to the level where they had been in December. "I feel like we're still in catch-up mode," Susan said. "Usually January and February is the time where kids take off in school. Especially you see it in first graders. This is where they really put reading together." She was quick to add, however, that both students and teachers had been very resilient and flexible.

As winter turned to spring, it was easy to see that the resilience and flexibility was getting students through the year. The Conant High boys' basketball team went on to win its class championship for the fourth year in a row, and the girls made it to the semifinals. Despite lost preparation time, several Jaffrey-Rindge creative problem-solving teams in the world-wide "Destination ImagiNation" program went on to place first in the state.

Another immediate concern for many, apart from getting the kids back in school, was replacing property damaged in the storm. Cars crushed by fallen limbs had to be replaced, and houses hit by trees had to be mended as well. Among the most notorious restorations, however, was home water damage from burst pipes.

Jim Sterling of Sterling Quality Cleaners in Keene specializes in drying out houses after natural disasters. Having been in the business for 30 years, he said the December ice storm brought him more calls than he had ever seen. When I spoke to him early in May, Jim said his company was still receiving calls about ice storm-related mold damage.

During the months following the storm, Jim hired additional help and ramped up his business, accommodating 50 to 60 percent more than usual. And usually, those are the months he is his busiest anyway. Working on homes and businesses within a 100-mile radius of Keene, his company took on work in Massachusetts and Vermont as well as New Hampshire. "We were working seven days a week for two and a half months," Jim told me. "We have never worked that much for that long a period."

In addition to sucking out standing water and drying out homes with their industrial-sized dehumidifiers, Jim's company cleans up soot from fires and, as was common with the ice storm, improperly used heating systems. The worst-case scenario, which Jim said he saw many times, would be a house where people were not home

*This tree in Nelson, New Hampshire, photographed on December 13,
lost a large limb to the storm.*

for a week or two: Water pipes broke, floors warped with damage
to ceilings and walls, and "drop ceilings" would be altogether piled
on the floor. Some also had mold growing from floor to ceiling. "For
water damage, you don't ever have a total loss because you can gut
a house," Jim said. "But the damage devastates the people, because

we're not talking about ceilings and walls; we're talking about taking all of their belongings to a dumpster." While it was devastating for many, one silver lining for some was that insurance companies often covered Jim's services, preferring to dry structures early rather than deal with mold issues later.

While some people had difficulty collecting from insurance companies, at least one insurance representative tried to bend the rules to make lives easier for ice storm victims. A Nelson, New Hampshire, resident said early in May that her husband was at first reluctant to call for insurance money, thinking the family would not qualify. But in the end, he was glad he did. "He called and the guy asked if anything on the house got damaged, and the answer was no," she said. "But he was really good. The guy said, '10 days without power. You must have lost a lot of food in the freezer.' My husband said we don't keep much meat in the freezer and the guy said, 'No, you *must* have lost about $250 worth of food in the freezer.' Then, bang, they sent us a check. That's going to pay for a professional to take care of a tree. That was good."

Insurance came through for municipalities as well. The Federal Emergency Management Agency (FEMA) made disaster declarations in the southern counties of Bennington and Windham in Vermont; in the western, northern, and northeastern counties of Berkshire, Franklin, Hampden, Hampshire, Worcester, Essex, and Middlesex in Massachusetts; in the southern counties of Androscoggin, Cumberland, Knox, Lincoln, Sagadahoc, Waldo, and York in Maine; in the southeastern counties, excluding New York City, of Albany, Chenango, Columbia, Delaware, Dutchess, Greene, Orange, Otsego, Putnam, Rensselaer, Saratoga, Schenectady, Schoharie, Sullivan, Ulster, and Washington in New York; and in the entire state of New Hampshire. This allowed municipalities within those counties to receive 75 percent federal aid for damages incurred during the storm. Although FEMA did not extend aid to individuals or businesses, it was a relief to know that local tax money would be saved.

Then there were the damages beyond money and time impossible to quantify. Following the storm and subsequent outages, people were physically drained and mentally anxious. Each weather report predicting severe snow or ice sent some into a panic.

There was absolutely no consensus among the people I spoke with about whether global warming or climate change had anything to do with the ice storm. People were split evenly on both sides of the issue, but it certainly played into some people's fears that the December 2008 ice storm was a part of a climate trend.

The River Center, a community resource center in Peterborough, offered a group session with a mental health professional early in March. Erika Bingham, a board member at the River Center, organized the event after receiving multiple calls from people having trouble following the ice storm. "It was not during the big storm with the outages, it was shortly after that," Erika said. "During another storm on the 5th of January, people started calling expressing concerns. They were going to Market Basket in Rindge, and there were lines out the door with people trying to stock up supplies. Their anxiety was that they had never seen Market Basket closed before," as it had been during the storm.

The more calls she received, the more she likened the experiences she was hearing about to a post-traumatic situation. It was not just a select group of people calling – those living alone or those without income – she was receiving calls from people of all income and education levels. She said this was particularly eye-opening given that the New Englanders she is used to dealing with are normally quiet and private about their troubles.

Erika related a story about how even talking about the normally ubiquitous subject of the weather set off a friend of hers more than a month after the storm was over. She had been out of power for more than 10 days. "When we were talking about snow, her eyes welled up with tears," Erika said. "For her, the idea of lugging the water up to the house, the idea of starting all over with that, it overwhelmed her. I think people get overwhelmed by the prospect of having to do that all over again."

About a month before the ice storm, fellow *Ledger-Transcript* reporter Meghan Pierce won the New Hampshire Press Association's "Writer of the Year" for news reporting in a weekly publication, but she said it was too emotional to sit down and write about the ice storm, even though it was her job. "You couldn't go anywhere without people telling you what they had been through," Meghan said. "People didn't want to talk to you as a reporter; they wanted to talk as a person. I just wanted to turn it off and be a human."

One of the most terrifying moments for Meghan, a Peterborough resident, was driving through Jaffrey and Rindge to get to Ashby, Massachusetts, to pick up her brother's car. He had gotten a flat tire while driving during the night of the ice storm and could not

Trees and limbs litter the ground at Monadnock State Park in Jaffrey, New Hampshire, following the ice storm.

change it because the lug nuts were frozen. Police drove him back to the station where the dispatcher let him borrow her personal car to get the rest of the way home.

When Meghan headed to Ashby the day after the storm, it was the afternoon, and wires and poles were all over the road without a highway department worker in sight. "It was frightening that it was the afternoon and still no one is cleaning this up," she said. "There were barriers on the roads. That was scary, but it was scarier that there was all this electric stuff hanging all over the place and trees hanging on wires. I picked him up and I was almost out of gas. There was nowhere to get gas on the way. I thought there would be gas somewhere."

A single mom, Meghan made the choice to live in Peterborough to be close to her family. The problem was that when catastrophe struck, everyone was in the same boat. Following the ice storm, she said she had thoughts of moving out of the area. "I felt like I was all alone; I could have been anywhere and it didn't help me that I was around family," she said. "There was nothing I could do for my parents; there was nothing they could do for me. They ended up spending a night at the South Meadow School shelter, and I stayed at a neighbor's house. I could be doing that anywhere in the world."

In April, I visited a real estate agent in Jaffrey who I was told had received many calls from people trying to get out of the Monadnock region after the storm. Intrigued, I stopped by and asked if this was true. The woman behind the desk gave me a strange look. "I think people in the Monadnock region are a little heartier than that!" she said, denying that she had an unusual number of homes for sale. I never heard of anyone leaving the region as a result of the ice storm.

The final components of the recovery effort were the trees themselves. Much of the work that was to be done necessitated waiting until the snow melted, but some of the effects were felt before then, most notably in maple syrup production. Chris Pfeil of The Maple Guys in Lyndeborough, New Hampshire, said the first time he looked at one of his orchards he found it to be a total loss. Tree tops were snapped and the tubing system he and his partner had rigged to tap trees was destroyed and buried.

Chris has been in the business for 10 years, and his business mindset is constant expansion. The Maple Guys syrup business grew every year it was in existence until the 2008-2009 season, when it had to settle for staying even. Money for a large expansion was redirected into restoration and working to get the company back to where it was the year before. "It could have been a lot worse," he said.

In neighboring Temple, New Hampshire, Ben's Sugar Shack went from 4,500 taps to 700, and the 700 produced less than a quarter of what those same taps did the year before when owner Ben Fisk said he had produced 1,140 gallons of syrup. The year of the ice storm, the Temple production was 38 gallons.

Like Chris and The Maple Guys, Ben found a way to keep making syrup, renting a sugar shack that had been on the market in Newbury, New Hampshire, and producing 825 more gallons there. While the ice storm devastated his crop for the following season, Ben said he was confident that he would stay in business in the coming years, getting back up to 4,000 taps in Temple and working with the Newbury location as well. "The leaves are on the trees now, so I can tell what's going to make it and what's not," Ben said. "I can restore it; it's just going to take a lot of hard work and time, making the cost to make it go up higher."

Spring came early following the storm, and through the month

A moving van is among the cars driving on Route 101 in Dublin, New Hampshire, with ice-covered wires and trees above."

of April, property owners and road workers began the mammoth task of gathering the fallen brush and stacking it roadside. Small piles were built up along every road. Town and state officials tried to get this done quickly, fearing outbreaks of forest fires with so much wood on the ground.

New Hampshire Fire Marshal J. William Degnan said early in May that he was not as worried about a major forest fire from the storm as he was about the danger hanging limbs continued to pose for people in the woods for recreation or to clean up. "In the town of Bedford, there was a tree leaning on a house and a woman came out and wound up getting pinned under the tree," he said. "That kind of exposure is the greatest risk as people work to clean up after the storm. Branches can fall because of high wind, and it's going to take some time to flush some of those out. They can be hung on those trees just by a thread."

The biggest danger of a fire was roadside, the fire marshal said, where there was the greatest amount of damage and where a careless motorist might toss a cigarette butt or where a car accident could spark a fire with additional fuel. Such fires were not more likely, he said, but would be more dangerous if they occurred.

In some places, collecting the debris was a relatively simple process of making a schedule to do certain roads, but in others, such as Worcester, Massachusetts, additional problems delayed the cleanup. Faced with a recent outbreak of the Asian Long-Horned Beetle, Worcester faced restrictions in dealing with wood and cutting down trees before the ice storm hit.

The Asian Long-Horned Beetle is native to China and other parts of the Far East, and its appearance in Massachusetts was distressing to agricultural groups because of its devastating effects on maple and other species of trees. As a result, tree limbs that fell in Worcester following the ice storm were stuck in Worcester. "That continues to be problematic," said Massachusetts Emergency Management spokesman Peter Judge of the potentially beetle-infested limbs. "This will go on for months. They can't move them. There are all kinds of United States Department of Agriculture restrictions there."

One of the most epic cleanups in the Monadnock region was on Mount Monadnock itself. On the mountain there were more than 30 miles of trails that had to be cleared, many of which had become indistinguishable from the surrounding woods, even to the rangers who knew them like their own back yard.

For park manager Patrick Hummel, the trails were his back yard. Patrick stayed at the Monadnock State Park base camp throughout the storm-caused power outage. Sitting in the darkness, his thoughts were mostly about reopening the park, or at least a portion of it, as soon as possible. "I didn't have the luxury of sitting back and evaluating each trail," Patrick said. "But I had pretty well accepted that we'd start on the White Dot and White Cross trails, the two most frequently climbed."

Wanting to avoid cutting through trees off the trail and creating a confusing network of dead ends, Patrick and his crew worked slowly and deliberately. Weather conditions after the storm did not help. The snow and cold temperatures slowed the work in the winter and the increased use of the trails slowed the work in the spring. Despite these challenges, the popular White Dot and White Cross trails were opened to hikers in mid-January, just a month after the storm.

Three-quarters of the mountain was left devastated with downed trees, but despite this overwhelming project, Patrick was adamant that only park rangers and those with intimate knowledge of the mountain trails work on their restoration. "We didn't rush," Patrick said. "We made sure the trails were all being done correctly with the debris being put in the right place. We couldn't let a group of 20 random people from the public do the work out there. It was a misconception among some people that it would have been cleared in a weekend."

The work itself involved far more than throwing sticks off of the trails, although that was a big part of it. The restoration required a great deal of chainsaw use, some with heavy trees, hanging branches, and layers of fallen trees snarled into each other. The crew would ideally consist of a chainsaw operator, someone to clear the debris by hand, and two handsaw operators, but most days it consisted of only two or three people. Five or six park rangers put in hundreds of hours, and by the end of April, all of the trails were open.

Originally from Brooklyn, New York, Patrick's family moved to the Monadnock region when he was 5 years old. While he spent his childhood more obsessed with baseball than the outdoors, he eventually came around to the mountain, first climbing it when he was 10 years old. After nine years working on the mountain, he became park manager in August of 2008, starting his tenure with the busiest foliage season the mountain had experienced in 10 years, followed by the December ice storm.

For Patrick and nearly everyone else in the Monadnock region, the "Mountain That Stands Alone" holds a special place in their hearts. Seeing the devastation on his favorite trails had a devastating effect on Patrick as well. "It was not only that it was my responsibility to clean it, but just the effects on the trails," he said. "It was heart-breaking." Patrick continued that the images of the trails prior to the ice storm are burned into his mind, and the changes he has seen since the storm are changes for the worse. "I don't know if my attitude will change over time as far as whether the sadness will shift more toward that pride in being able to turn this mountain back into hikable condition," he said. "Some of the sadness may go away over time, but I don't know if that 'Wow' factor will ever decrease."

One of the most impressive restoration stories came from the Cathedral of the Pines, an outdoor sanctuary in Rindge, New Hampshire, created in 1945 on a plot of land where Sanderson Sloane planned to build his home after returning home from World War II. Sanderson never came home, and his parents, Douglas and Sybil, erected the sanctuary in his honor. They dedicated it to inclusion of all faiths and as a memorial to military service with a message of universal peace. The sanctuary overlooks Mount Monadnock, a view that was originally opened up due to damage from the hurricane of 1938. A seating area was constructed among the pines growing on the property, and for more than 60 years, marriages, memorial services, and religious events of all kinds took place under the shade of those trees.

Then came the Ice Storm of December 2008.

Following the storm, trees long weakened by excessive foot traffic and maintenance of the sanctuary were a complete loss. Hundreds of them toppled or were too damaged to save, and what was once an outdoor sanctuary became a pile of debris. Gone were the pines of the Cathedral of the Pines.

According to executive director Allen Clapp, couples came over to the site during the week afterward to scope out the damage. Many lamented, and some burst into tears seeing the devastation to what had been their wedding place or special to them in some other way. While the damage was immense, Allen did see a silver lining. The open sanctuary had become even more open, revealing a richer view of the mountain. Just as the hurricane had opened the partial view of Monadnock, the December ice storm finished the job. He went to work almost immediately on the Cathedral's restoration. In his words, it was more than a restoration; it was a rebirth.

On March 25, after all the tree stumps had been removed, landscape architect George Hayward came in to mastermind a plan for the new sanctuary. The goal was to complete the project by the Cathedral's opening date of May 1, just over five weeks away. As a result of collaboration among many local contractors, paths were carved, stone walls were erected, seating was built, an underground sound system was installed, and flowers and shrubs were planted, along with nine new pine trees. "It does not have the majestic pines scattered through the seating area, but the absence of those trees has enhanced the view and made the Cathedral what it is," Allen said shortly after the work was completed, taken aback by the result. "This is more like a theater now." Facing the ever-present "Altar of the Nation," dedicated to the men and women who gave their lives in an effort for peace, two levels of seating have a wide open view of Mount Monadnock. The work was finished on May 1, 2009.

Dorrie Upton was emotionally overcome to see the new sanctuary. She had been married there many years before and saw it directly after the storm. She did not know if the sanctuary would still have the same sense of peace without the canopy of pines, but

The Cathedral of the Pines in Rindge, New Hampshire, saw hundreds of the pines it is named for come down as a result of the storm.

seeing the place after May 1 was her answer. "I could not stop the tears from flowing," Dorrie said. "They were tears of joy."

Like the Cathedral of the Pines, all locations affected by the storm are recovering one way or another, some changed in appearance, with leaning trunks and missing branches in plain sight. But whether the ice storm was a chance at rebirth or, as for most, a huge inconvenience to endure, the people affected pressed on. And while the ice storm of December of 2008 bent the backs of a geographic region, it would not break them.

What the ice storm did do was renew the reality of catastrophe to the Northeast. As the nearly 100-year-old Doris "Granny D" Haddock remarked, commenting on the 70 years between the ice storm and the previous widespread disaster of the hurricane of 1938, "You never know when it is going to happen again."

An ice covered flower in Guilford, Vermont, on December 12.

Ice Storm Fact Sheet

HOUSEHOLDS WITHOUT POWER

New Hampshire: 420,000
Massachusetts: 350,000
New York: 300,000
Maine: 230,000
Vermont: 40,000
TOTAL: 1,340,000

COUNTIES ELIGIBLE FOR FEDERAL AID

New Hampshire: All

Massachusetts: Berkshire, Essex, Franklin, Hampden, Hampshire, Middlesex, Worcester

New York: Albany, Chenango, Columbia, Delaware, Dutchess, Greene, Orange, Otsego, Putnam, Rensselaer, Saratoga, Schenectady, Schoharie, Sullivan, Ulster, Washington

Maine: Androscoggin, Cumberland, Knox, Lincoln, Sagadahoc, Waldo, York

Vermont: Bennington, Windham

PUBLIC SERVICE OF NEW HAMPSHIRE

1,300 transformers replaced
13,600 fuses installed
780 utility poles replaced
105 miles of wire restrung
408,000 service calls
1,700 employees called into service
1,205 work crews from in state and out
$75,000,000 spent

Two hikers observe ice-covered wonders on Pinnacle Mountain in Lyndeborough, New Hampshire, on December 12.

Acknowledgements

First and foremost, I would like to thank Craig Brandon, owner of Surry Cottage Books, whose belief in this project transformed it from an idea to a reality.

My aunt Ingrid Eisenstadter, who likes when I call her Beautiful Tante Ingrid (BTI), was instrumental during the editing process, as were Steve Leone, Jane Eklund, and my father, Peter Eisenstadter (who I'm sure was assisted by my mom, Susan Loman, in opening e-mail attachments).

Many thanks to Michel Newkirk, who fit working on this book cover into her busy graphics schedule. It's a cover I don't mind people judging the book by. Thanks also to Martin Murray and PSNH for helping secure permission for the cover photo and others throughout the book. Anya Rose was the creative mastermind behind some of cover concepts, and deserves special thanks, as well.

Thank you to the staff at the Peterborough Town Library, the Keene Public Library, and the Frost Free Library for assisting with research. And a huge thanks goes to the staff of Brewbaker's Coffee Shop and Bagel Works (The Works Café) for not kicking me out during my frequent writing sessions at their tables.

Thank you to Heather McKernan, publisher of the *Monadnock Ledger-Transcript*, for her support of this project, and to the entire staff of the *Ledger-Transcript*, whose journalistic diligence during the ice storm and at other times is an inspiration.

I really must also thank Jeff Petrovitch, whose attempts at time management coaching met with mixed results. Lisa Weiss and Danner Claflin also offered welcome support, often at short notice.

Of course, everyone who gave me an interview and/or submitted pictures and/or pointed me in someone else's direction deserves thanks, as well. I hope not to leave out too many of you, and my apologies if I do. Thanks to Erika Bingham, Andrew Freeman, Michelle Bishop, Tracie Smith, Rick Edmunds, Scott Oliver, Terra MacLean, Frank LaGrande, Norm Sturgeon, Brenda Zavattero, Shane Vanderbilt, M'lue Zahner, Melissa Lee, Chris Pfeil, Liz Hardison, Jack Burnett, Pam Crook, Mike Stone, Bill Burt, Michael Miller, David Poirier, Camelia Sousa, Kendra McGhee, Ben Fisk, Dave Westover, Donna Robertson, Heather Atwell, Jim Sterling, Steve Boucher, Patrick Hummel, Geoff Jones, Laura Gingras, Colin Manning, Meghan Pierce, Dave Anderson, Marcia Patten, Roland Patten, Jacobe Trudelle, Thane Page, Dick Bergeron, Susan Copley, Marian Alese, Tim Grossi, Richard Dunning, Niki McGettigan, Kenyon Acton, Chris Lund, Craig Hicks, Henry Bley-Vroman, Scott Tolman, Michaela Tolman, Deb Giaimo, Fred Giaimo, Doris "Granny D" Haddock, Kirsten O'Connell, Allen Clapp, Jan Heirtzler, Terry Varney, Cynthia Geary, Glenn Coppelman, Alexandra Gardner, Jenn Lund, Leigh Libby, Adam Heintz, Bruce Griffin, Debbie Lindsey, Ray Lindsey, Don Freeman, Margaret Freeman, Emma Stamas, Jeremy Stamas, Emily Sauter, George Griffin, Bruce Griffin, Marguerite Durant, John Matesowicz, Rebecca Karam, Brendan Tapley, Karen Sampson, Glenn Joziatis, Victor Reno, Kent Koeninger, Matt Cohen, Elizabeth Williams, Paul Landry, Marilyn Vose, Elice Laughner, Lisa Sieverts, Max Nunnemaker, Bob Lepp, Stephanie Fitzpatrick, Jami Landry, Tali Fridman, Beth Krommes, Ashley Pushkarewicz, Jay Starr, Mitch Call, Don Primrose, Louise Rath, Dan Rath, Sue Marland, Steve Fisher, Debbie Fisher, Jose Macias, Bobbie Petrovitch, Sarah Cooper-Ellis, Margritt Richter, Siggy Richter, Phil Schlichting, Chris Young, Laura Fletcher, Ron Reed, Mike Dailey, Tracy Lee Carroll, Liz McGovern, Jeff Newcomer, Ogion Fulford, Ron Waterman, Tiger Waterman, Aaron Howland, Deborah Idaka, Yuichi Idaka, Oscar Hills, Patti Hills, Steve Lindsey, Lisa Cody, Peter Judge, Jim Van Dongen, J. William Degnan, Dennis Michalski, Barbara Farr, Neal Cass, Larry Kullgren, Steve Weber, Garrett Chamberlain, Elizabeth Thomas, Rodney Bartlett, Peggi Brogan, Peter Crane, Joe Dellicarpini, Hayden Frank, Tim Carpenter, Ashley Daige, BJ Wahl, Julie Rossall, Massey and Tomlinson Photography, Ben Kimball, Jack Rodolico, Dave Letourneau, David Hayes, Eric Lasky, Thomas Walton, Catherine Boeckmann, David Blair, Alison Scott, Mary Wesley, Sally Wright, Lynette Miller, Robert McAleer, Linden Rayton, Emily Wheelwright, Steven Fisher, Amanda Borozinski, John Koch, Carol Kender-McNiff, Kristin Valente-Blanchard, Justin Rhody, Mary Beth D'Aloia, Geoff Forester, Doris Burke, Natalie Dennen, Brittany Bartlett, Paul Madalinski, Eneida Maisonave, Laurie Redfern Smith, Jonathan Smith, Linda Lawrence, Rainy Stanford, Sal Clark, Ron Dion, Linda Odell, Kelly Roy, Dania Strong, Joy Chipman, Kevin Morris, Tom Chaloux, Emily Ashman, Nicholas Runco, Virginia Manning, Rose Crittendon, Tamra Veilleux, Bob Viarengo, and Dana Denison.

Photo Credits

Page 6: Geoff Forester for PSNH
Page 9: Ashley Daige
Page 10: Max Nunnemaker
Page 13: Dave Anderson
Page 14: Ogion Fulford
Page 17: Linda Odell
Page 18(top): Patti Hills
Page 18(bottom): Patti Hills
Page 20: Natalie Dennen
Page 22: Joe Dellicarpini
Page 23: Catherine Boeckmann
Page 24: Ron and Tiger Waterman
Page 26: Carol Kender-McNiff
Page 28: Pam Crook
Page 30: BJ Wahl
Page 32: Peggy Lambert
Page 34: Geoff Forester for PSNH
Page 35: Ron Dion
Page 36: Diana Strong
Page 37: Dana Denison
Page 39: Adam Katrick
Page 40: Marilyn Vose
Page 42: Fred Giaimo
Page 43: Glenn Joziatis
Page 44: Catherine Boeckmann
Page 45: Doris Burke, PSNH
Page 46: BJ Wahl
Page 48: Ashley Daige
Page 50: Catherine Boeckmann
Page 51: Catherine Boeckmann
Page 52: Carol Kender-McNiff
Page 53: Linda Lawrence
Page 54: Max Nunnemaker
Page 55: Dave Eisenstadter
Page 56: M'Lue Zahnder
Page 57: Peggy Lambert
Page 58: Geoff Forester for PSNH
Page 59: Julie Rossall
Page 60: BJ Wahl
Page 61: Ron and Tiger Waterman
Page 64: Max Nunnemaker
Page 66: Carol Kender-McNiff
Page 67(top): Catherine Boeckmann
Page 67(bottom): Amber Fields
Page 68(top): Natalie Dennen
Page 68(bottom): Sal Clark
Page 69(top): Steven Fisher
Page 69(bottom): Ron and Tiger Waterman
Page 70: BJ Wahl
Page 72: Jeff Newcomer
Page 74: BJ Wahl
Page 78: Photo courtesy Kirsten O'Connell
Page 80: Mike Dailey
Page 83: Dave Eisenstadter
Page 84: Ron and Tiger Waterman

Page 86: BJ Wahl
Page 87: Dave Eisenstadter
Page 88: Rose A. Crittendon
Page 90: Ben Kimball
Page 93: Max Nunnemaker
Page 94: Photo courtesy PSNH
Page 95: Photo courtesy PSNH
Page 96: Ron and Tiger Waterman
Page 100: Dave Eisenstadter
Page 102: BJ Wahl
Page 105: Linda Lawrence
Page 107: Dave Eisenstadter
Page 110: Dave Eisenstadter
Page 112: Ogion Fulford
Page 113: Ogion Fulford
Page 115: Sue Copley
Page 118: Peggi Brogan
Page 123: Peggi Brogan
Page 124: Carol Kender-McNiff
Page 126: Ogion Fulford
Page 128: Joy Chipman
Page 130: Doris Burke, PSNH
Page 132: Ashley Daige
Page 134: Dave Eisenstadter
Page 135: Dave Eisenstadter
Page 136: Paul Madalinski
Page 137: Geoff Forester for PSNH
Page 138: Natalie Dennen
Page 139: Doris Burke, PSNH
Page 140: Doris Burke, PSNH
Page 141: Doris Burke, PSNH
Page 142: Doris Burke, PSNH
Page 143: Doris Burke, PSNH
Page 144: Doris Burke, PSNH
Page 145: Ron and Tiger Waterman
Page 148: Ogion Fulford
Page 150: Kelly Roy
Page 151: Mary Beth D'Aloia
Page 153: Pam Crook
Page 154: Dave Eisenstadter
Page 156: Scott Oliver
Page 158: Amber Fields
Page 159: Natalie Dennen
Page 164: Dave Eisenstadter
Page 166: Peggy Lambert
Page 168: Dave Eisenstadter
Page 169: Ashley Daige
Page 172: Max Nunnemaker
Page 175: Peggy Lambert
Page 177: Julie Rossall
Page 181: Photo courtesy Cathedral of the Pines
Page 182: Ogion Fulford
Page 184: Amber Fields

Index